TAKE-ALONG
Knitting

20+ easy portable projects from your favorite authors

WITH PATTERNS BY

STEFANIE JAPEL, PRUDENCE MAPSTONE, HANNAH FETTIG AND MORE

NORTH LIGHT BOOKS

Cincinnati, Ohio

www.mycraftivity.com
Create. Connect. Explore.

Knitting

20+ easy portable projects from
your favorite authors

WITH PATTERNS BY
STEFANIE JAPEL, PRUDENCE MAPSTONE,
HANNAH FETTIG AND MORE

Other fine North Light Books are available from your local bookstore, art supply store or direct from the publisher.

13 12 11 10 09   5 4 3 2 1

DISTRIBUTED IN CANADA BY FRASER DIRECT
100 Armstrong Avenue
Georgetown, ON, Canada L7G 5S4
Tel: (905) 877-4411

DISTRIBUTED IN THE U.K. AND EUROPE BY DAVID & CHARLES
Brunel House, Newton Abbot, Devon, TQ12 4PU, England
Tel: (+44) 1626 323200, Fax: (+44) 1626 323319
Email: postmaster@davidandcharles.co.uk

DISTRIBUTED IN AUSTRALIA BY CAPRICORN LINK
P.O. Box 704, S. Windsor NSW, 2756 Australia
Tel: (02) 4577-3555

Library of Congress Cataloging in Publication Data
Take-along knitting : 20+ easy portable projects from your favorite authors / by Heidi Boyd ... [et al.]. – 1st ed.
    p. cm.
  Includes index.
  ISBN-13: 978-1-4403-0538-2 (pbk. : alk. paper)
  ISBN-10: 1-4403-0538-2 (pbk. : alk. paper)
 1. Knitting. 2. Knitting–Patterns. I. Boyd, Heidi, 1966-
TT825.T28 2010
746.43'2041–dc22

                            2009039616

media
www.fwmedia.com

Editor: Rachel Scheller

Layout Editor: Layne Vanover

Designer: Geoff Raker

Production Coordinator: Greg Nock

Photographers: John Carrico, Ric Deliantoni, Tim Grondin, Adam Henry, Adam Leigh-Manuell, Stephen Murello, Al Parrish, Christine Polomsky, Brian Steege, Lorna Yabsley

Metric Conversion Chart

to convert	to	multiply by
Inches	Centimeters	2.54
Centimeters	Inches	0.4
Feet	Centimeters	30.5
Centimeters	Feet	0.03
Yards	Meters	0.9
Meters	Yards	1.1
Sq. Inches	Sq. Centimeters	6.45
Sq. Centimeters	Sq. Inches	0.16
Sq. Feet	Sq. Meters	0.09
Sq. Meters	Sq. Feet	10.8
Sq. Yards	Sq. Meters	0.8
Sq. Meters	Sq. Yards	1.2
Pounds	Kilograms	0.45
Kilograms	Pounds	2.2
Ounces	Grams	28.3
Grams	Ounces	0.035

This book features patterns from these great F+W Media, Inc. titles:

Soft + Simple Knits for Little Ones
— Heidi Boyd —

Knitted Sock Sensations
— Louise Butt and Kirstie McLeod —

Spin Dye Stitch
— Jennifer Claydon —

Knit One, Embellish Too
— Cosette Cornelius-Bates —

Pints and Purls
— Karida Collins and Libby Bruce —

Beautiful Embroidered & Embellished Knits
— Jane Davis —

Felting The Complete Guide
— Jane Davis —

Closely Knit
— Hannah Fettig —

Knitted Wire Jewelry
— Samantha Lopez —

Glam Knits
— Stefanie Japel —

The Knitchicks' Guide to Sweaters
— Marcelle Karp and Pauline Wall —

Freeform Style
— Jonelle Raffino and Prudence Mapstone —

Knitting the Perfect Pair
— Dorothy Ratigan —

Contents

Introduction

As an avid and enthusiastic knitter, I tend to take my current projects everywhere I go. Family and friends have often teased me about my tendency to break out the needles on buses and planes, in restaurants and waiting rooms, at baseball games and band concerts—even in the supermarket. It's as if my fingers are constantly itching to cast on and create, the present situation or location notwithstanding.

I like to think that I'm not alone. I believe there are plenty of knitters out there who share the sentiment that knitting is an "anytime" endeavor. It is from this belief that *Take-Along Knitting* was born.

In this book you will find patterns from some of our finest and most respected knitwear designers: Jane Davis, Stefanie Japel, Hannah Fettig, Heidi Boyd and more. These projects were specially selected because they are truly portable. You'll find fast-knitting scarves, gloves and hats, as well as a few bags and even a baby sweater. The combination of ease, sumptuous yarn and classic design is what makes these projects some of the best we've ever published. The best part, though, is that you can take them anywhere you'll have two free hands and a bit of time.

In addition to the patterns, I've gathered a series of tips and tricks to make on-the-go knitting easier. From basic knitting techniques you'll need for every project to helpful hints for traveling with your yarn and needles, these suggestions will prove invaluable the next time you feel the urge to knit and purl in public.

So, if you feel, as I do, that knitting can and should be taken anywhere, this book is for you. And if you've never knitted in public before, I urge you to try it. Who knows? Perhaps the knitting you take along will inspire someone else to pick up the needles, too.

Happy knitting!

—Rachel Scheller | *Editor, North Light Books*

Chapter 1

Getting Started

Even the most experienced knitters need to refer to the basics every once in a while. Within this section you'll find an essential guide to knitting techniques, yarn characteristics, needles, notions and more. It's the perfect portable reference when a pattern stumps you, or when you just need a refresher course in Kitchener stitch or cabling.

We've included step-by-step guides for knitting and purling, as well as for more advanced techniques. There's even a tutorial on crochet. Better yet, these techniques were specially picked to coordinate with the projects in this book, so if you choose to take one of them along, you'll have all the information you need at your fingertips!

Needles

Needles in the Know

Knitting needles are manufactured from all sorts of materials. Try out a few pairs to see what you like best. You may find that some needles go better with certain types of fibers than others. For example, super-smooth needles plus super-smooth yarn equals slippery stitches that slide easily from needle to needle. Squeaky acrylic on grabby bamboo may lead to stubborn stitches that refuse to slide along the needles.

Needle tips also come in different shapes. Wood and bamboo needle tips tend to be stubby, while metal needles often have more streamlined tips. The pointiest of all needles are those made for lace knitting, although they can be used for any project. Following are descriptions of the most common knitting needle materials:

Aluminum (nickel and nickel-plated): These needles are turbo charged! Yarn glides along the metal so smoothly and quickly that many call these the fastest needles around.

Bamboo: Always dependable, bamboo needles are light and a bit flexible. Bamboo is a sustainable resource, so it's probably the most environmentally conscious choice.

Casein: These needles are made of organic materials. Casein is a protein found in milk. Go green!

Glass: Clear or brightly colored, these needles are functional works of art and are surprisingly strong.

Plastic: These needles are the most economical choice, and they're good for learning. Bryspun brand plastic needles are recommended for knitters with arthritis. Watch out—plastic needles can snap more easily than needles made from other materials.

Wood: Beautiful and smooth, wood needles are a real treat! Wood needles are often made of birch, ebony or rosewood, but they can also be cherry, maple or walnut.

Needles Are Us

Different knitting projects require different types of needles. The three basic kinds of needles are straight, circular and double-pointed. Each type of needle is suited to a particular type of knitting. Choose what works best for you.

Straight: The most iconic knitting implement, these needles come as a matching pair of two straight sticks in varying lengths with a flattened knob at one end to stop the knitting from sliding off.

Circular: The real workhorse of handknitting, circular needles are two needle tips connected by a flexible cord generally made of nylon. Use circular needles to knit in the round or to knit large projects back and forth so the weight of the knitting rests in your lap instead of being supported by your wrists. You can purchase circular needles in interchangeable sets that allow you to create whatever size needle you want connected with whatever length of cord you desire.

Double-pointed: Double-pointed needles come in a set of four or five, and they're used to knit small pieces in the round, such as sleeves, socks or the tops of hats.

The Needle Size Chart

Knitters work a great deal with charts. Here is one of many you will encounter in this book: The metric/US needle size chart. The US has its own system, while the rest of the world uses metric.

Metric (in mm)	US	Metric (in mm)	US
1.0	000	6.0	10
1.5	00	6.5	10½
2.0	0	7.0	
2.25	1	7.5	
2.5		8.0	11
2.75	2	8.5	
3.0		9.0	13
3.25	3	9.5	
3.5	4	10.0	15
3.75	5	12.75	17
4.0	6	16.0	19
4.5	7	19.0	35
5.0	8	20.0	36
5.5	9	25.0	50

Size Me Up

Needles come in all different lengths and thicknesses. This can get confusing because there are generally three numbers attached to size, all of which typically appear on the needle.

Diameter: A needle's diameter is measured in millimeters. The US size is given as a corresponding number.

Shaft: How long is this needle anyway? The length of the needle is usually given on the needle packaging. For circular needles, the length is measured from tip to tip and includes the joining cord.

Yarn

Yarn is the umbrella term we use for all types of knitting fibers. Sheep's wool is the most well-known fiber spun into yarn, but it's really just a small part of what's available today. We get a lot of yarn from other animals as well, including goats, rabbits, alpacas, camels and silkworms. Cotton, linen and hemp are all-natural plant cellulose, while viscose takes natural materials and adds chemical elements. Technology has also given us completely artificial yarn that is a byproduct of petroleum: polyester. Add combinations or blends of fibers, and you end up with an almost endless range of yarns.

How Do You Choose?

Knitting patterns always recommend a type of yarn or even a specific brand. This recommendation is in no way random, as the designers take the properties of the yarn into consideration when designing a garment. For instance, you probably won't see a cashmere summer T-shirt, because cashmere is wonderfully warm. When you're knitting from a pattern, the safest bet is to use the exact yarn listed. If you plan to substitute a different yarn, you should choose one with similar properties.

Animal Fibers

Alpaca: Indigenous to South America, the alpaca is part of the camel family (it's often confused with a llama). Lightweight and silky, like human hair, alpaca has no fluff.

Angora: The Angora rabbit produces the fiber used to make this yarn, which has a fluffy halo. Angora fiber is very soft, and yarns made from it can shed.

Cashmere: This fine, light, soft and warm fiber is taken from the undercoat (not guard hair) of the cashmere goat, a breed that originated in the Himalayas. It's quite expensive!

Mohair: Strong, elastic, shiny and fluffy, this wool-like fiber comes from the Angora goat.

Merino: Merino fiber is wool fiber that comes from the merino breed of sheep. It's the finest and softest variety of wool.

Silk: This shiny, soft fiber actually comes from a protein filament spun by the silkworm to form its cocoon.

Plant Fibers

Cotton: Cotton yarn is spun from plant cellulose. It can be hard on the fingers, but it produces a breathable fabric.

Linen: This durable and lightweight fiber comes from the flax plant.

Bamboo: A relatively new player on the fiber scene, bamboo fiber is made from cellulose in the bamboo stalk. Bamboo fiber has properties similar to linen and cotton, plus it has nifty antibacterial properties.

Synthetic Fibers

Polyester: This artificial fiber is very strong and easy to wash—you can throw it in the washing machine.

Rayon: This soft yarn drapes well, but it has no stretch at all! Rayon comes from processed wood pulp called viscose. Bamboo fiber is also processed with a chemical in a similar fashion.

Blends

Blends are a great way to get the best of all worlds! For example, a 50 percent wool and 50 percent polyester blend creates a woolly yet strong yarn that can be thrown in the washing machine. Mixing cashmere with other fibers creates soft yarn that's more affordable and easier to maintain. Combining a fluffy fiber such as angora with another fiber ensures it sheds less. The combinations are endless.

Types of Yarn

The choice of yarn does not end with the fiber. The way this fiber is spun or produced (processed) is also important.

Ply: A ply is a single strand of yarn. Most yarns are made of multiple, twined plies. For example, a two-ply yarn is made up of two strands.

Spiral/twist: To make fiber into yarn, it must be spun. When the fiber is created by twisting it to the left, it's called an S twist. When twisted to the right, it's a Z twist.

Bouclé: This yarn has a knobbly look created by one of its multiple strands being longer than the others.

Chenille: This fuzzy yarn has a thick woven core with short fibers around it.

Tape/ribbon: Just as the name suggests, this is flat yarn.

Cabled: Multiple-ply yarn that is plied together is called cabled yarn.

Slub: Irregular in shape, slub yarn is thick and thin in different spots.

It's Not Heavy, It's Yarn

Despite the name, "yarn weight" doesn't mean how much a ball weighs. Rather it refers to the thickness of the yarn. Yarns range from strands so fine it looks like you could floss your teeth with it to so chunky you could almost wrap it around your neck as a scarf without even bothering to knit it.

There are many systems of labeling yarn weight that seem to differ according to where you live. The Antipodeans use a ply method, the United Kingdom and United States have individual systems that sometimes use crossover words with differing meanings, and there's no system at all on the continent. The Craft Yarn Council of America has instituted a nomenclature to even things up (*Vogue Knitting* uses this in its patterns), but it has not been universally adopted.

The Craft Yarn Council of America issues many helpful charts on their Web site (www.craftyarncouncil.com), and the Standard Weight System shown below is no exception. Gauge is given over 4" (10cm) of Stockinette stitch.

	Super Bulky (6)	Bulky (5)	Medium (4)	Light (3)	Fine (2)	Superfine (1)	Lace (0)
Type	bulky, roving	chunky, craft, rug	worsted, afghan, aran	DK, light worsted	sport, baby	sock, fingering, baby	fingering, 10-count crochet thread
Knit Gauge Range	6–11 sts	12–15 sts	16–20 sts	21–24 sts	23–26 sts	27–32 sts	33–40 sts
Recommended Needle in US Size Range	11 and larger	9 to 11	7 to 9	5 to 7	3 to 5	1 to 3	000 to 1

Considering Gauge

So what does all this mean when you're choosing yarn for your project? It means you'll have to carefully choose a yarn-and-needle combination that produces the gauge recommended in the pattern. If you don't match up your gauge to the recommended gauge in the pattern, you'll have to recalculate to get the correct numbers of stitches and rows. Depending on the tension of your knitting, the gauge can change. Which is why—that's right, here comes the broken record—it's important to check your gauge by knitting a swatch with your yarn and needles of choice per project.

The Yarn Label

There's a wealth of information on the yarn label, and it's there for a reason: to guide you. Take note of the following information given on the yarn label and compare it to your pattern:

- Manufacturer
- Name of yarn
- Fiber content
- Actual weight
- Length (yardage)
- Recommended needle and gauge
- Shade
- Dye lot
- Care instructions

Here's a tip: When purchasing multiple skeins of yarn, make sure all the yarn comes from the same dye lot—there can be subtle differences in color that might not be obvious to the naked eye but will definitely show up midsweater.

But There's No Label

What if you've lost the label, bought it from a local producer or just can't read the language? Use the Wraps Per Inch (WPI) method of determining weight (most commonly used by spinners). To do this, wrap the yarn around a WPI tool, a pencil or similar, ensuring that the yarn is evenly spaced, with each strand touching the next (not too loose and not too tight). Now measure this against a ruler or check it against a Wraps Per Inch chart.

Ply	Yarn Weight	St/inch	WPI
2-ply	lace, laceweight	33–40	18+
3-ply	superfine, fingering, sock	27–32	16
4-ply	fine, baby, sport	23–26	14
8-ply	light, DK, sport/light worsted	21–24	12
10-ply	medium, aran, worsted	16–20	11
12-ply	heavy worsted	17–18	11
14-ply	chunky, bulky	12–15	10
15+-ply	bulky, superbulky	6–11	8

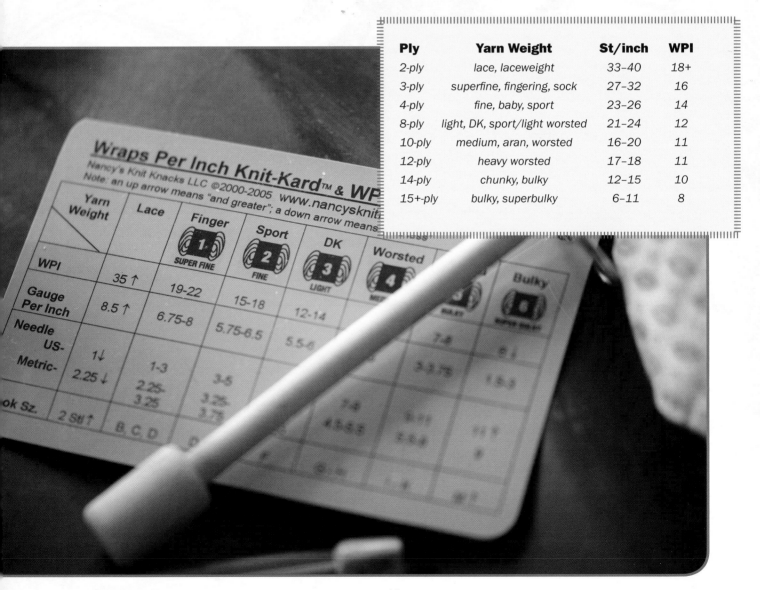

Notions

Bobbins: When you're battling intarsia, bobbins are the go-to to keep the yarn from tangling. The trick is to let them dangle behind the work. Wrapping yarn around a piece of cardboard or a barrette can work perfectly as a homemade bobbin.

Cable hooks: These U-shaped or hook-shaped needles are used to hold stitches when we're working cables.

Crochet hooks: Yes, we are knitters, but on occasion we'll go to our sister craft to help with threading fringes, fine-tuning edges, making picot embellishments and picking up dropped stitches.

Gauge ruler: These compact rulers measure knit stitches over 4" (10cm). Many gauge rulers also contain holes for needle sizing.

Journals: We use journals to keep track of our schedules, so why not keep copious notes on our knitting habits? A well-kept knitting journal is a wonderful reference, short- and long-term!

Knitting bag: Knitting bags should be just big enough to carry your yarn and notions. Choose a bag that's not too deep so things are easy to grab. Velcro is a destroyer of multi-ply yarn, so avoid it in your knitting bag. There are many stylish and functional bags out on the market to choose from. Everyday handbags also work very well as knitting carry-alls, including backpacks.

Needle cases: For those of us shy about using a vase as a needle holder, you can use needle cases to hold straight needles, circular needles, DPNs and crochet hooks. Sturdy, economical needle cases are out there, ready for the purchasing.

Point protectors: You know how sometimes you reach into your bag to pull out your work and you pull the yarn off the needle instead? Point protectors stop this from happening; just stick them on the end of your needle. You can also use sponge bits that you cut yourself, a pencil eraser or a simple rubber band. A point protector can be placed on one end of a DPN to turn it into a short straight needle.

Pom-pom makers: These can be a goddess-send for those of us completely unable to create pom-poms. They're easy to work with, instead of all the fumbling you may endure otherwise; of course, you can make one of these yourself out of cardboard.

Pouches/minis: Small, zippered bags are wonderful for holding small accessories. Recycle makeup bags to carry around little notions or use zip-top freezer bags to corral buttons and such.

Row counters: For those of us who are easily distracted, row counters are a dream come true, as you are forced to pay attention to where you are at all times. They are as compact as most notions go, which is all you can ask for when you start piling up the notions quotient!

Scissors: There's snipping to be done when you are a knitter. As such, a small pair of scissors will come in handy. For those of you who travel, there are also notched yarn cutters; they look like flat buttons and are as sharp as a hairdresser's shears.

Stitch holders: Many knitters will use scrap yarn to function as a stitch holder, but you can also use the ones you find at your local yarn store. They will take good care of your live stitches!

Stitch markers: These round rings slip between your stitches on the needle. The thinner your stitch marker, the better. It's best to use the ones that clip on and off. Small pieces of yarn can be used as stitch markers, and safety pins work well, as they are quite thin. Think of stitch markers as your project's jewelry.

Tape measure: Well, we all know how important measuring is to your project, don't we? Even our grandmothers carried a tape measure around. This notion is one of the few musts on your list of notions.

Tapestry needles: They sound fancy, but they're basically sewing needles with eyes large enough to accommodate the bulkiest of yarns. They're excellent seaming devices and are not at all sharp.

17

Casting On ⧓⧓⧓⧓⧓⧓⧓⧓⧓⧓⧓⧓⧓⧓⧓⧓⧓⧓⧓⧓⧓⧓⧓⧓⧓

There are several different methods that can be followed to cast on, and each one produces slightly different results. Here are two of the most common cast-on methods.

Long-Tail Cast On

This is the most common way to cast on stitches. It might seem a little awkward to hold the yarn this way and hook the needle tip through each loop, but once you get the hang of it, you'll be amazed at how quickly the stitches add up. This technique creates a nice, clean cast-on edge at the bottom of your knitting.

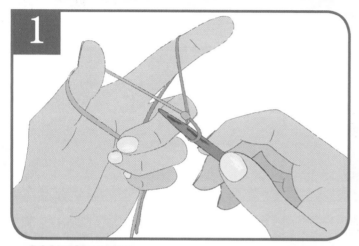

POSITION YARN

Make a slip knot, leaving a long tail (at least 4" [10cm] for every 1" [3cm] you'll be casting on). Slide the slip knot onto the needle with the long tail toward the front of the needle. Slide your thumb and index finger between the two strands of yarn. Wrap the long tail around your thumb and the strand still attached to the skein around your index finger. Grasp both strands with your remaining fingers.

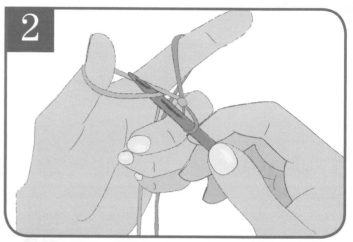

BRING NEEDLE THROUGH FRONT LOOP

Slide the tip of the needle up through the loop of yarn wrapped around your thumb.

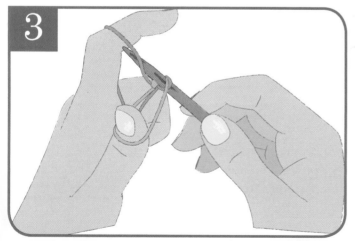

CATCH SECOND STRAND

Keeping the needle in the loop of yarn around the thumb, hook the needle behind the strand of yarn on the front of your index finger.

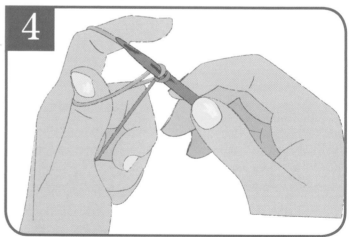

DRAW BACK STRAND THROUGH FRONT LOOP

Bring the yarn through the loop of yarn on your thumb, creating a second loop on your needle (the first cast-on stitch). Gently tug on the strands with thumb and index finger to tighten the cast-on stitch. Repeat to cast on the remaining stitches. Include the slip knot in your stitch count.

Backward-Loop Cast On

This is the simplest cast-on method to learn, but it does not provide the most stable edge. Use this cast-on method to close the body of a mitten or mitt into a round after the thumb stitches have been split from the knitting.

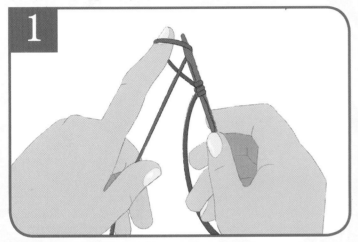

CREATE LOOP

Make a slip knot and slide it onto a knitting needle. Loop the working yarn around your index finger. Insert the tip of the knitting needle into the loop.

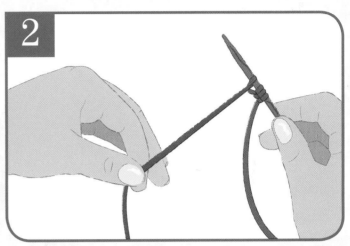

TIGHTEN LOOP

Tighten the loop around your needle by gently pulling on the working yarn until the newly added stitch is snug on the needle. Repeat to cast on the remaining stitches. Include the slip knot in your stitch count.

Take-Along Tip

Before casting on for a project you'll be taking with you, consider your needle choice. Aluminum and metal needles are more slippery than bamboo, wood or plastic; if you stuff a scarf into your purse that's attached to aluminum needles, the stitches might slip off. Point protectors are the traveling knitter's best friend; they can be bought in nearly every needle size and prevent stitches from escaping the needles.

If you plan to knit on a plane during a long flight, keep in mind that particularly sharp needles might have to go in your checked luggage. Pack blunt needles instead and save yourself the worry. Keep in mind that metal scissors and thread cutters are currently prohibited on planes. To snip a long cast-on tail, pack a pair of nail clippers.

Knitting Continental

When knitting continental, hold the yarn around your left index finger and dip the right-hand needle tip into it before making a stitch.

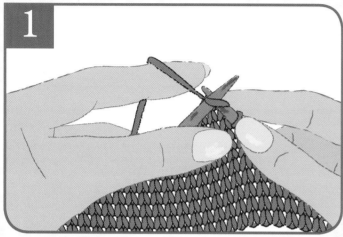

1 POSITION NEEDLES

With the working yarn wrapped over your left index finger, insert the right-hand needle into the first stitch on the left-hand needle from front to back. The right-hand needle should cross behind the left-hand needle.

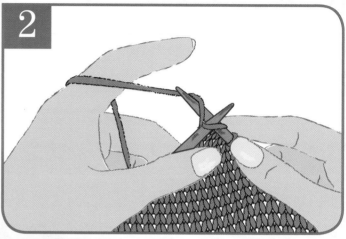

2 WRAP YARN

Bring the right-hand needle tip behind the yarn in front of your left index finger. The working yarn should be wrapped around the right needle tip counterclockwise.

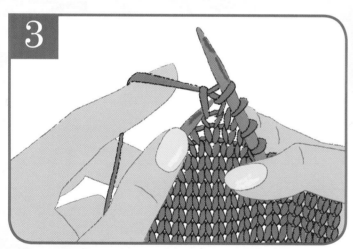

3 CREATE NEW STITCH

Dip the needle tip down and pull the wrapped yarn through the stitch on the left-hand needle. Bring the yarn up on the right-hand needle to create a new stitch, allowing the old stitch to slide easily off the left-hand needle. The new stitch remains on the right-hand needle.

Purling Continental

Purling continental offers all the same advantages as knitting continental. Purled rows are easily distinguished by the raised wavy pattern.

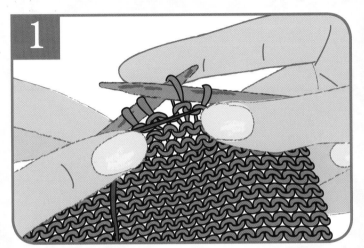

POSITION NEEDLES

With the working yarn in your left hand, slide the tip of the right-hand needle into the first stitch on the left-hand needle from back to front. The right-hand needle should cross in front of the left-hand needle.

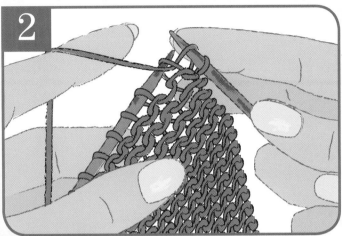

WRAP YARN

Use your left hand to wrap the working yarn around the tip of the right-hand needle counterclockwise. Draw the right-hand needle back through the stitch on the left-hand needle, catching the wrapped working yarn with the tip of the needle. Bring the working yarn through the stitch on the left-hand needle.

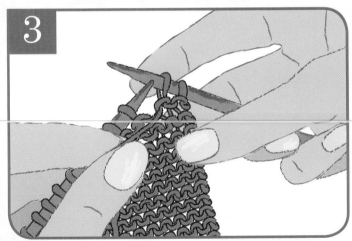

CREATE PURL STITCH

Bring the yarn up on the right-hand needle to create a new stitch, allowing the old stitch to slide off the left-hand needle. The new stitch remains on the right-hand needle.

For illustration purposes, the working yarn is shown held between the index finger and thumb. However, when working a row of purl stitches, the yarn should remain in the position shown in Step 2 to create proper tension.

Joining Stitches

When knitting in the round, stitches are cast on in the usual manner and then joined with a knit stitch to form a circle.

Joining with a Circular Needle

Circular needles make knitting in the round almost effortless.
Cast on, join the stitches and off you go!

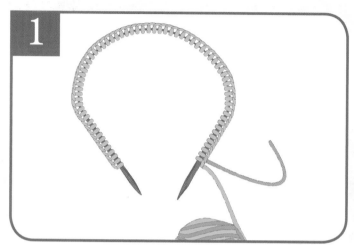

CAST ON STITCHES

Cast on the required number of stitches and spread them evenly around the length of the circular needle. Lay the needle down on a flat surface with the working yarn on the right and the points of the needles facing you. Carefully straighten the cast-on row so that the bottom of each stitch is on the outside of the circular needle and none of the stitches are twisted over.

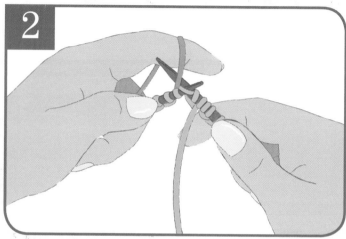

JOIN STITCHES

To join the stitches for working in the round, insert the right-hand needle into the first stitch on the left-hand needle from front to back. The right-hand needle should cross behind the left-hand needle. Pull the working yarn through to make a new stitch as usual.

Joining with Double-Pointed Needles

When you first start knitting with double-pointed needles, you may feel like you're playing a game of Pick Up Sticks, but put a little work into learning this technique, and you will be rewarded for the rest of your knitting life!

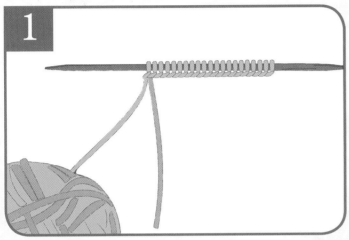

CAST ON STITCHES

Cast on the required number of stitches onto one double-pointed needle.

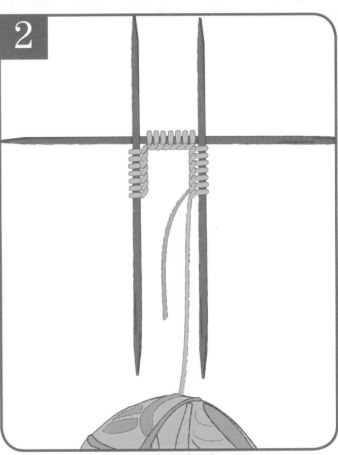

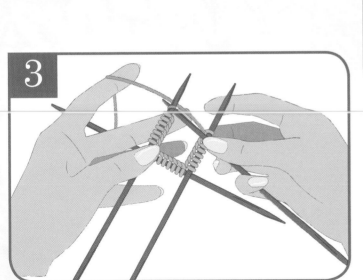

JOIN STITCHES

Hold the needle with the working yarn in your right hand and the needle with the first cast-on stitch in your left hand. Insert the tip of the free needle into the first cast-on stitch. Wrap the working yarn around the tip of the free needle and knit the first stitch as usual.

DISTRIBUTE STITCHES

Divide the cast-on stitches as evenly as possible among the double-pointed needles. If you are using a set of four double-pointed needles, distribute the stitches over three needles, leaving one needle for working. If you are using a set of five double-pointed needles, distribute the stitches over four needles, leaving one needle for working. When dividing the stitches, slip the stitches onto the new needle as if to purl; otherwise, your cast-on row will have twisted stitches. Lay the needles down on a flat surface with the working yarn on the right. Carefully straighten the cast-on row so that the bottom of each stitch is toward the inside of the needles and none of the stitches are twisted over.

Increasing and Decreasing

Increasing and decreasing allow you to shape your knitting to any size. Eliminating stitches makes the piece smaller, and adding stitches makes the piece larger. Once you've familiarized yourself with these basic shaping techniques, you're ready to shape any pattern.

Knit Two Together (k2tog)

This technique really is as simple as it sounds. By placing your needle tip through two stitches instead of one, you knit the stitches together into a single stitch.

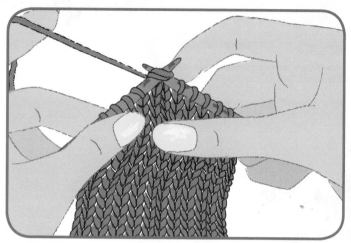

Slide the right-hand needle into two stitches together from front to back, as for a regular knit stitch. Knit the two stitches together as one stitch. This will lower your stitch count by one stitch. When the two stitches have been knitted together, you will see that the decrease leans to the right.

Pass Slipped Stitch Over (psso)

This technique creates a left-leaning decrease that is usually paired with a k2tog to create a centered double decrease.

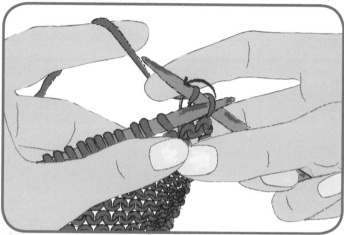

Insert the left-hand needle into the second stitch from the tip of the right-hand needle. Pull that stitch over the first stitch at the end of the right-hand needle and off the right-hand needle. This will lower your stitch count by one stitch.

Slip, Slip, Knit (ssk)

The ssk is the left-leaning symmetrical sister of k2tog that brings perfect shapely symmetry to your knitted piece.

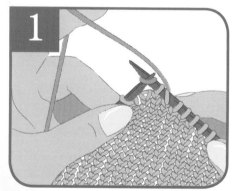

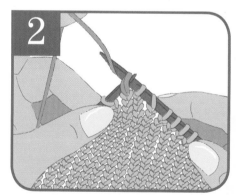

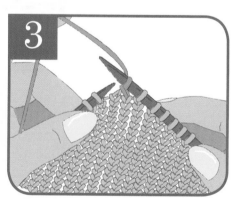

SLIP STITCHES

Insert the tip of the right-hand needle into the first stitch on the left-hand needle as if to knit. Slip the stitch off the left-hand needle onto the right-hand needle. Repeat with a second stitch.

POSITION NEEDLES

Insert the left-hand needle into the fronts of both slipped stitches. The left-hand needle should cross in front of the right-hand needle. Wrap the working yarn around the right-hand needle counterclockwise.

KNIT STITCHES TOGETHER

Knit the two stitches together as one stitch. This will lower your stitch count by one stitch. When the two stitches have been knitted together, you will see that the decrease leans to the left.

Knit One Front and Back (kfb)

The title of this technique explains the process very clearly. By knitting a single stitch twice you create two stitches where there used to be one.

KNIT INTO FRONT OF STITCH

Slip the right-hand needle into the first stitch on the left-hand needle from front to back and knit the stitch as usual, but do not slip the stitch off the left-hand needle.

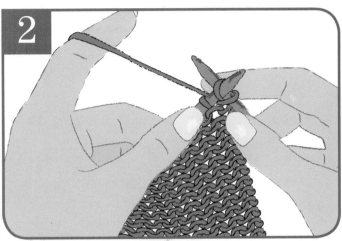

KNIT INTO BACK OF STITCH

Insert the right-hand needle through the back of the same stitch and knit another stitch.

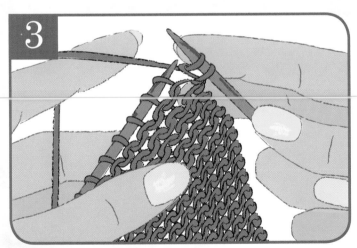

CREATE NEW STITCH

Slide the old stitch off the left-hand needle. The right-hand needle should now have two new stitches. This will increase your stitch count by one stitch.

Make One Left (m1l)

This increase creates a defined line of stitches that slants to the left.

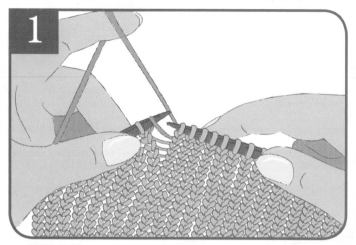

LIFT BAR

Bring the tip of the left-hand needle under the strand between stitches from front to back.

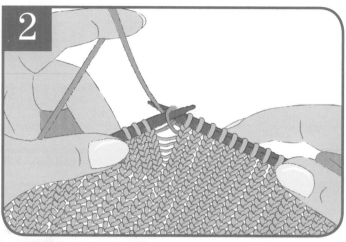

POSITION NEEDLES

Insert the tip of the right-hand needle through the back of the yarn sitting on the left-hand needle.

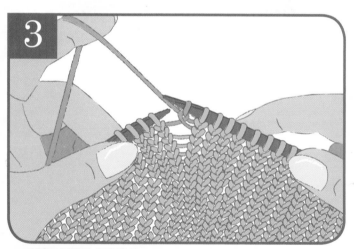

KNIT NEW STITCH

Knit this strand through the back loop to twist it. The right-hand needle should now have a new stitch. This will increase your stitch count by one stitch.

Make One Right (m1r)

This increase creates a defined line of stitches that slants to the right.

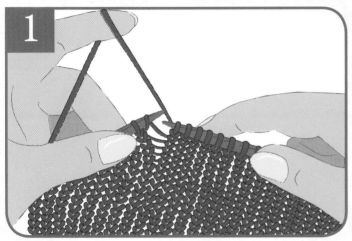

LIFT BAR

Bring the tip of the left-hand needle under the strand between stitches from back to front.

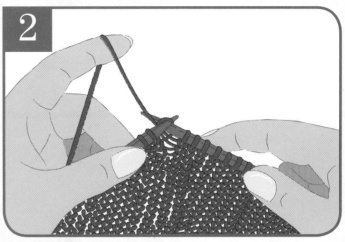

POSITION NEEDLES

Insert the tip of the right-hand needle through the front of the yarn sitting on the left-hand needle. The right-hand needle should cross behind the left-hand needle.

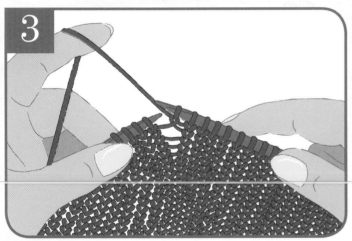

KNIT NEW STITCH

Knit this strand through the front loop to twist it. The right-hand needle should now have a new stitch. This will increase your stitch count by one stitch.

Binding Off

All good things must come to an end so they can be worn. Obviously, you can't just slip live stitches off your needle; if you did, your work would completely unravel. To finish off your knitting properly, you must bind off your stitches in one of the following ways.

Traditional Binding Off

This binding off process loops one stitch into another, stabilizing the edge of your work. It's very important to be aware of your tension while binding off. If you pull the stitches too tightly, you can pucker the top of your knitting and restrict its ability to stretch.

KNIT TWO STITCHES

Knit the first two stitches in the row just as you would for a normal knitted row.

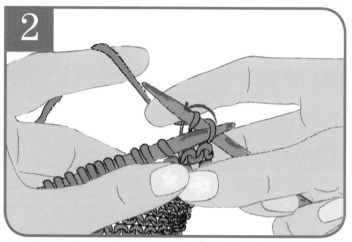

PASS FIRST STITCH OVER SECOND STITCH

Insert the left-hand needle into the first knitted stitch on the right-hand needle and pass it over the second knitted stitch on the right-hand needle.

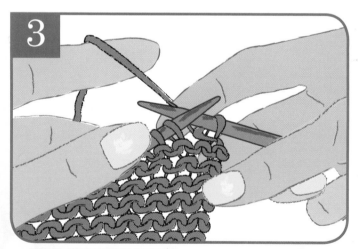

BIND OFF FIRST STITCH

One stitch will remain on the right-hand needle.

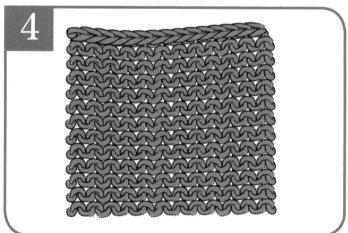

BIND OFF REMAINING STITCHES

To bind off the next stitch, knit one stitch (two stitches on right-hand needle) and then pass the preceding stitch over the newly knitted stitch. Continue to knit one stitch and then pass the preceding stitch over it until you have bound off all the stitches. Cut the yarn and pull the tail through the final stitch.

Three-Needle Bind Off

This technique is for binding off two pieces of knitting together to form a seam. Stitches are arranged evenly on two needles, and a third needle is used to knit a stitch from each needle together and then bind them off.

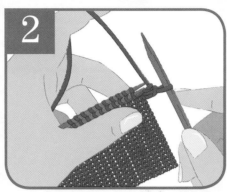

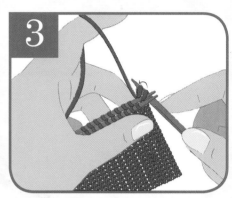

POSITION STITCHES

Transfer your stitches evenly to two straight needles. Make sure the working yarn is at the pointed end of the needle. Holding the two needles together in your left hand, insert a third needle through the first stitch on each left-hand needle from front to back. The right-hand needle should cross behind both left-hand needles. Wrap the working yarn around the tip of the right-hand needle.

KNIT STITCHES

Knit the two stitches together as one stitch. Repeat Steps 1 and 2 to knit a second stitch.

BIND OFF FIRST STITCH

Insert one of the left-hand needles into the first stitch on the right-hand needle and pass it over the second knitted stitch on the right-hand needle. To bind off the next stitch, repeat Steps 1 and 2 to knit another stitch (two stitches on the right-hand needle) and then pass the preceding stitch over the newly knitted stitch. Continue to knit one stitch and then pass the preceding stitch over it until you have bound off all the stitches. Cut the yarn and pull the tail through the final stitch.

Closing the Top of Circular Knitting

This technique is not technically a way to bind off stitches but is a way to finish your knitting and secure your stitches.

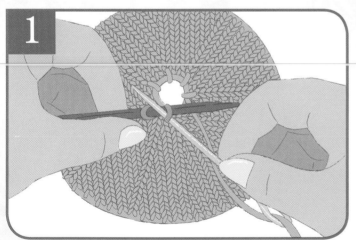

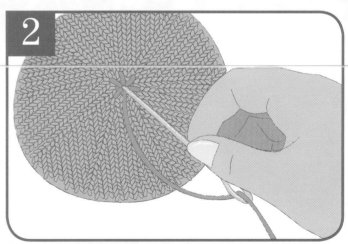

SLIP STITCHES

After working the last round of the pattern, cut the working yarn, leaving at least a 6" (15cm) tail. Thread the yarn tail through the eye of a tapestry needle. Slip all stitches on the knitting needles onto the tapestry needle.

TIGHTEN STITCHES

Pull the yarn tail through the stitches, tightening the stitches until there is no gap at the closing point. Insert the tapestry needle into the center of the tightened stitches, pull the tail through to the inside of the knitting and knot it. Weave the tail into the wrong side of the knitting to secure it.

Seaming With Kitchener Stitch

Use Kitchener stitch any time you need to join two rows of knitted loops together. Kitchener stitch, when done correctly, looks like just another row of knitting and is as perfectly elastic as your knitted fabric.

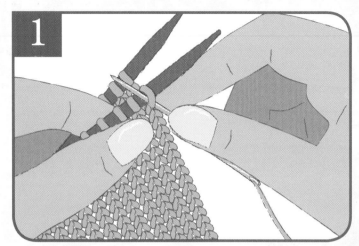

MAKE FIRST SETUP STITCH

Transfer the stitches to be seamed evenly onto two straight needles. Make sure the working yarn is at the pointed end of the needle. Thread a tapestry needle with yarn. Hold the two needles together in your left hand with the wrong sides facing inward and the right sides facing outward. Insert the threaded tapestry needle into the first stitch on the left-hand needle closest to you as if to purl. Pull the tapestry needle through the stitch, leaving the stitch on the needle.

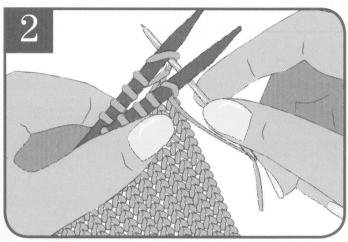

MAKE SECOND SETUP STITCH

Insert the tapestry needle into the first stitch on the left-hand needle farthest from you as if to knit. Pull the tapestry needle through the stitch, leaving the stitch on the needle.

Steps 1 and 2 are done only to set up for seaming. Once these preparatory stitches are complete, the rest of the stitches will be seamed in the following pattern: knit, purl, purl, knit.

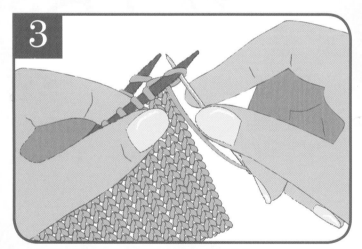

SLIP STITCH FROM FRONT NEEDLE

Insert the tapestry needle again into the first stitch on the front needle, this time as if to knit, while slipping it off the end of the needle.

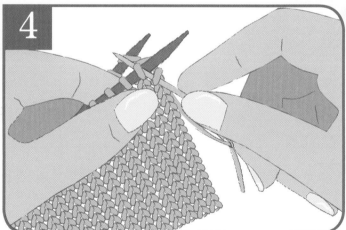

CONTINUE GRAFTING

Insert the threaded tapestry needle into the next stitch on the left-hand needle closest to you as if to purl. Pull the tapestry needle through the stitch, leaving the stitch on the needle. Pull the seaming yarn through the stitch, but do not excessively tighten the seam.

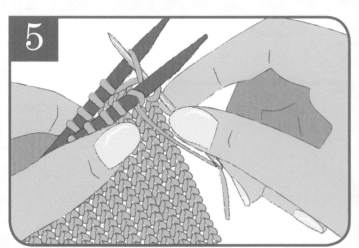

SLIP STITCH FROM BACK NEEDLE

Insert the tapestry needle again into the first stitch on the back needle, this time as if to purl, while slipping it off the end of the needle.

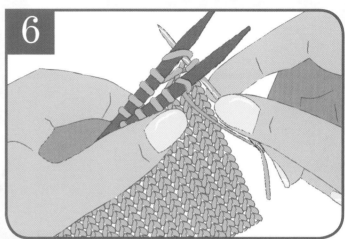

CONTINUE GRAFTING

Insert the threaded tapestry needle into the next stitch on the left-hand needle farthest from you as if to knit. Pull the tapestry needle through the stitch, leaving the stitch on the needle. Pull the seaming yarn through the stitch, but do not excessively tighten the seam.

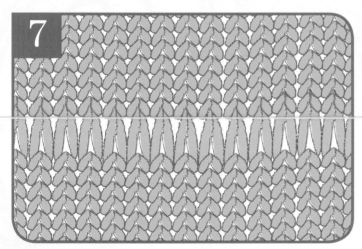

FINISH GRAFTING

Continue seaming until all the stitches are grafted together. The seaming yarn will appear loosely woven between the two rows of grafted stitches.

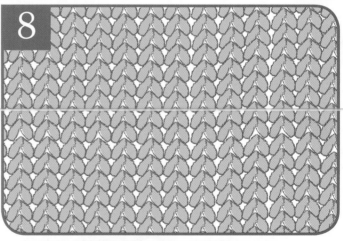

ADJUST TENSION OF SEAMING YARN

Lay the seamed fabric flat. Gently adjust the tension of the seaming yarn until it matches the tension of the knitted fabric. When the seaming yarn is properly tensioned, the seam should be invisible.

Picking Up Stitches

Making new stitches at the finished edge of a piece allows you to add new elements, such as earflaps, to your knitting. Picking up a stitch means you are creating new knitted stitches attached to the edge of the piece.

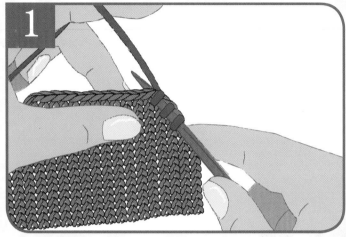

POSITION NEEDLE

Insert the tip of a knitting needle under a stitch on the finished edge of the knitted fabric. Be careful to pick up both strands of yarn from the stitch.

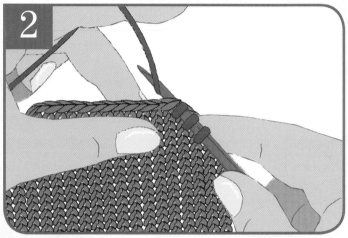

WRAP YARN

Wrap the working yarn around the tip of the needle counterclockwise, just as when knitting.

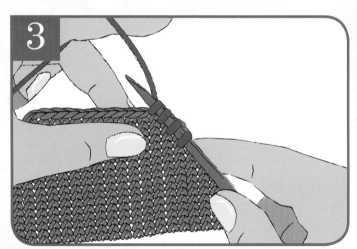

CREATE NEW STITCH

Using the tip of the needle, pull the yarn through the knitted fabric, creating a new stitch on the needle. Continue picking up stitches until the appropriate number of stitches is on your needle.

Knitting I-Cord

Use this technique to knit a three-dimensional piece without connecting the stitches. By simply sliding the stitches down to the other end of the double-pointed (or circular) needles, you force them to create a little tube. I-cords can be knitted in all different sizes and lengths and make handy ties, drawstrings, handles and even clever little topknots for stretchy hats.

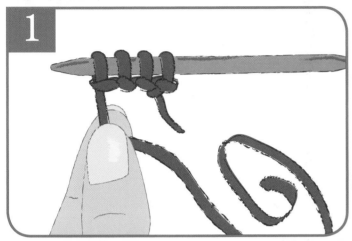

CAST ON STITCHES

Cast on the required number of stitches onto one double-pointed needle.

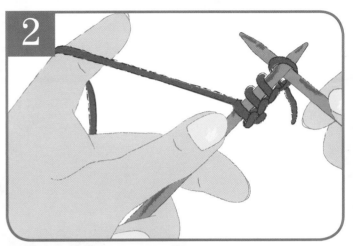

PREPARE FOR FIRST STITCH

Slide the stitches on the double-pointed needle so that the first cast-on stitch is at the right-hand point of the double-pointed needle and the working yarn is to the left of the stitches. Insert another double-pointed needle into the first cast-on stitch.

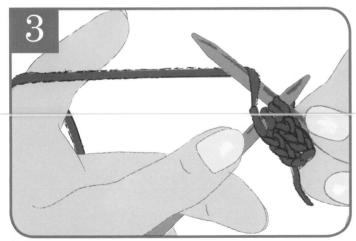

KNIT I-CORD

Pull the working yarn from the last stitch to the first stitch and knit. Knit all stitches in the first row. Instead of turning the needle when you finish a row as you would for regular knitting, simply slide all the stitches from the left point to the right point of the needle again. Do not turn your work at all while knitting I-cord. Keep pulling the working yarn behind the tube that forms to the first stitch in each row. After a few rows, you'll see the beginning of a knitted tube—without having purled a stitch, and without ever turning your work.

Cabling

Knitting cables involves making a "twist" in the knitted fabric. You do this by working stitches from a cable needle held either at the front (for a left cross) or the back (for a right cross) of the work. You can use either a short, straight double-pointed needle, or a special cable needle that has a "kink" in it to hold the stitches on. There are many cable designs, but here we've demonstrated the basic technique using Cable Four Front (C4F) and Cable Four Back (C4B).

Cable Four Front (C4F)

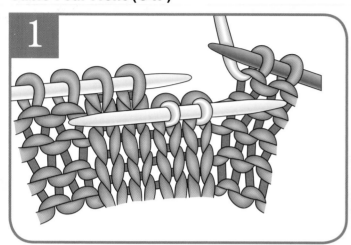

SLIP STITCHES ONTO CABLE NEEDLE

Work to the point where the cable twist is to be made. Slip the first two stitches on the left-hand needle onto your cable needle. Leave the cable needle hanging at the front of the work.

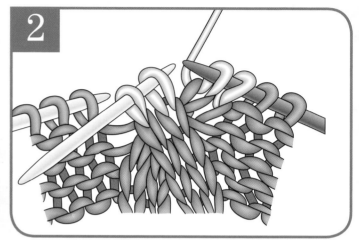

CREATE LEFT CROSS

Knit the next two stitches on the left-hand needle, using the right-hand needle as usual. Then knit the two stitches held on the cable needle. Put the cable needle aside and knit the rest of the row as usual.

Cable Four Back (C4B)

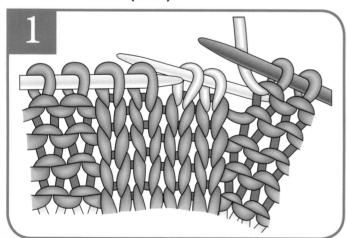

SLIP STITCHES ONTO CABLE NEEDLE

Work to the point where the cable twist is to be made. Slip the first two stitches on the left-hand needle onto your cable needle. Leave the cable needle hanging at the back of the work.

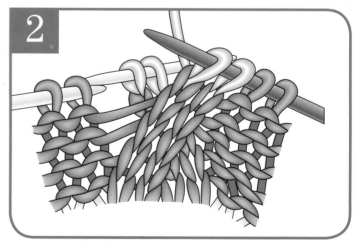

CREATE RIGHT CROSS

Knit the next two stitches on the left-hand needle, using the right-hand needle as usual. Then knit the two stitches held on the cable needle. Put the cable needle aside and knit the rest of the row as usual.

Intarsia

Changing colors and knitting images into your work is actually quite easy—it's just a matter of knitting stitches in a different color of yarn. To begin, wind a short length of accent color(s) onto a bobbin (or loop a length around your fingertips and then wind around the center of the loops). Following the color chart, switch to knitting from the bobbin/looped yarn for the required number of stitches. You'll find the intarsia patterns in this book are intended for beginners and only require one to two color changes. It's the perfect way to get started with this technique.

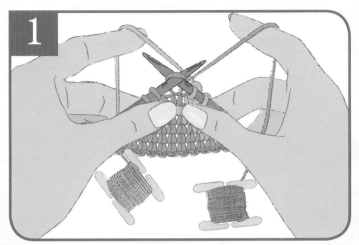

TWIST COLORS FROM RIGHT SIDE

When switching from one color to another with the right side facing, twist the old color and new color around each other behind the work to prevent gaps.

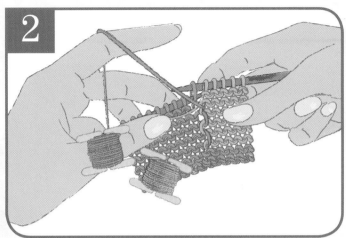

TWIST COLORS FROM WRONG SIDE

Twist the yarns around each other in the same manner when the back of the work is facing you.

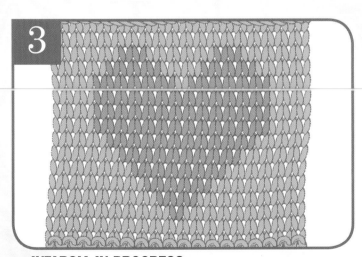

INTARSIA IN PROGRESS

From the front of the piece, your work will look like this as you progress. Notice the switches in color are seamless—there are no holes in the work. When weaving in the loose ends, be sure to weave them behind a matching color block so they're virtually invisible on both the front and the back.

Crocheting

Though this is a knitting book, some of the projects do require some basic crocheting skills (see *Hat and Soul* on page 64 and the *Fringed Scarf* on page 88). Crochet can also be used to embellish your knits as an edging or as a decorative stitch.

Chain Stitch

The chain is the first step of any crochet project. It's also just like a single knitted stitch that grows with every new loop of yarn.

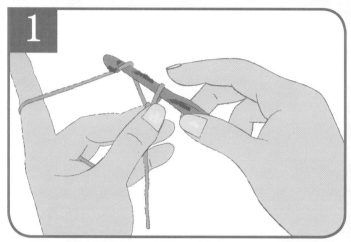

Make a slipknot at the free end of the yarn (the other end will be attached to the skein/ball). Slide the slipknot onto a crochet hook and then wrap the working yarn around the back of the hook clockwise.

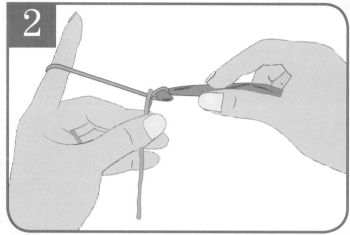

Move the hook so it grabs the wrapped working yarn and then pull the working yarn through the slipknot to form the first chain stitch.

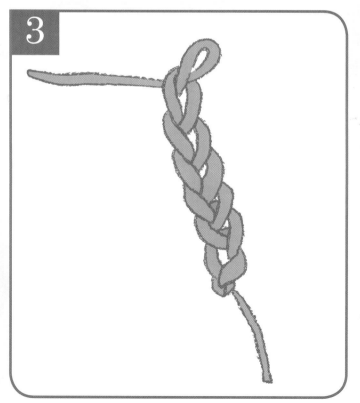

Continue to wrap the working yarn and pull it through each subsequent loop until the chain is the desired length.

Single Crochet

This type of stitch makes a neat row of compact stitches. If you're just beginning your work, you'll need to prepare a crochet chain or loop before making your first single crochet stitch.

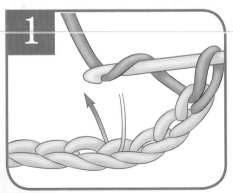

To begin the single crochet stitch, pass your hook through the closest stitch in the chain or the center of the loop. Wrap the yarn from front to back around the needle. Bring the hooked yarn back up through the stitch.

You should have two loops left on your hook. Wrap the yarn around the hook again and bring the yarn up through both loops. This completes your first single crochet stitch.

Double Crochet

The double crochet stitch is taller with a more lacy appearance. If you're just beginning your work, you'll need to prepare a crochet chain or loop before making your first double crochet stitch.

Start by wrapping the yarn front to back around the hook. Keep it wrapped while you pass the hook through the closest chain or center of the loop.

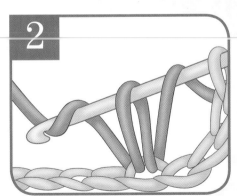

Wrap the yarn around the hook and bring it back up through the stitch. You'll now have three loops on your hook. Wrap the yarn around the hook again and bring it through the next two loops closest to the hook end.

Wrap the yarn around the hook a final time and bring it through the two remaining loops. This completes your first double crochet stitch.

Fulling Knitted and Crocheted Fabric

Knitted and crocheted items can be fulled to create a dense, fuzzy fabric. Fulling can transform a knitted or crocheted item into a much sturdier piece and is especially useful for items that need to be warm and hard-wearing like slippers, or for items that need to be dense, such as handbags, to keep the items inside from slipping out. Stiffening a fulled fabric with hat-stiffening products adds a new dimension to your work because you can make a piece hold a specific shape.

Hand Fulling

Hand fulling is the best technique to use with delicate crocheted and knitted items, as well as if you want to be able to monitor the progress of the fulling to achieve a certain size or appearance. All you need to get started is your knitted or crocheted fabric, a bowl or washtub of hot water, a bowl or washtub of cold water, dishwashing soap and a dry towel. You may also choose to use shaping tools, a cotton cord and a needle, but these items are optional.

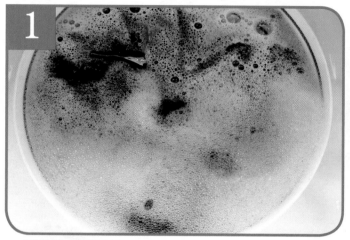

BEGIN FULLING

Prepare the edges of a piece if needed; the edges don't usually need to be prepared before hand fulling, though it can sometimes be helpful (see *Machine Fulling* on the next page). Soak the project in a bowl of very warm to hot water with 1 teaspoon of dishwashing soap until it is fully saturated.

FULL PROJECT

Knead the project with your hands until it fulls. To full by hand, remove the project from the warm, soapy water and knead it with your hands. When it cools, wet the project in warm, soapy water. Then plunge it into cold water and knead it some more to help full the project completely.

When the piece is fulled the desired amount, run it through cool water to rinse out the soap. Squeeze out the excess water and roll the piece up in a dry towel to remove as much of the water as possible. Shape the piece into its finished shape and let it dry. If you plan to drastically change the shape of the piece, let it dry and then steam it with a steam iron and pull it into its finished shape or dry the piece on a form.

Machine Fulling

Knitted and crocheted fabrics can be fulled by machine. Machine fulling is the faster, easier method, and most pieces can stand up to the high agitation level of machine fulling. However, the amount of fulling may be dictated by the settings of your washing machine. For this technique you'll need a washing machine and some dishwashing soap. Like before, however, you may choose to use shaping tools, a cotton cord and a needle.

PREPARE EDGES

Begin by preparing any exposed edges of the project so they won't stretch out of shape in the fulling process. Sometimes this is done during knitting or crocheting by working the last several rows in a nonfelting yarn or by decreasing the last few rows so the outside edges are smaller than the rest of the piece. I often baste openings closed with a cotton cord.

FIRST WASH CYCLE

Place the item in the washing machine on the hot wash/cold rinse cycle at the lowest water level. Add 1–2 teaspoons of dishwashing soap. You can also add an old pair of jeans, or other tough material that will not fade, for extra agitation. Don't put anything in the washer with your project that can shed fibers, such as towels, because the shed fibers will get imbedded in the fabric. Start the washing machine.

CHECK PROGRESS

Periodically stop the washer to see if your piece is fulled as much as you desire. In order to completely full an item, an entire machine cycle is usually needed. If the finished piece is meant to be worn, such as a hat, check approximately every five minutes to make sure the piece doesn't full too small or stretch out where it shouldn't.

FINISH PIECE

When the piece has shrunk down to size, run it through the rinse and spin cycles and then remove any basting stitches. Shape the piece into its finished shape and let it dry. If you plan to drastically change the shape of the piece, let it dry and then steam it with a steam iron and pull it into its finished shape or dry the piece on a form.

Drawstring Closure

If you want a drawstring closure on a project, you can knit or crochet the piece without adding holes and then string a shoelace through the stitches a few rows down from the top edge. Tie the ends of the shoelace together and throw the piece in the washer. This will eliminate the need to baste the openings or work holes into the pattern stitches.

Adding Embellishments

Beads

Finding and choosing beads for a project is an adventure in itself. Look for beads that you like and that go with the yarns you've chosen for your project, rather than trying to get the exact same beads used in the sample projects. There is a multitude of bead shapes, colors and finishes to choose from, so be sure to take your yarn with you to the bead store and hold them up to each other so you can visualize the finished project.

When choosing beads, keep in mind that delicate knitting can't carry the weight of a lot of heavy beads, so choose small beads for lightweight knitting. Also, bead holes vary in size, so make sure your beads have holes big enough for your needle and thread. Moreover, some beads are unique, so be sure to purchase enough for your project or ask if they are reorderable.

To attach beads to your knitting projects, always pierce the knitted stitches for each stitch so that the beads stay on the front of the knitted fabric, unless instructed otherwise, or when the knitting is tight enough to hold the beads on the front, as described in *Adding Beads Over Knitted Stitches* on the next page.

Attaching a Bead Dangle

Dangles can be added to the edge of knitting to make a fringe, or on the surface of the knitting for an accent.

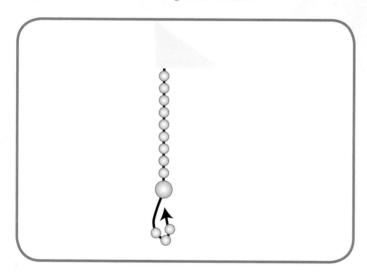

Attach the thread where you want the dangle to hang. String your chosen bead pattern, skip one or more of the last beads strung and pass the needle back up through the rest of the beads until you reach the knitting again. Before pulling the needle through the beads, slide the beads along the needle by pulling the needle toward you. This makes sure you haven't pierced the thread already in the beads. Now, hold on to the skipped beads with one hand and pull the thread through (this helps make sure you pull all of the thread through evenly). Take a small stitch in the knitting and pull the thread almost all the way through so a small loop forms. Pass the needle through the loop and then finish pulling the thread snugly so a small knot forms to lock the dangle in place.

Attaching Leaf Beads

This technique is for adding individual leaves on the surface of the knitting.

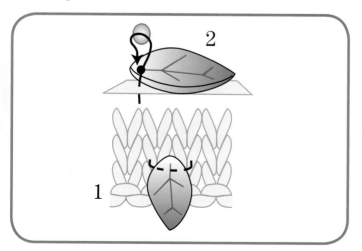

Come up from the back of the knitting and string a leaf bead. If the bead hole passes through the side of the bead, simply pass back down through the knitting, making a stitch the width of the bead (1). If the hole passes through the leaf from front to back, string a small round bead, such as a size 11 seed bead, and pass back down through the leaf bead and through the knitting in the same place where you originally came up through the knitting (2).

Looped Bead Edging

A beaded edge can be worked either around the knitted stitches or through them with piercing.

Stitching Beads in a Line

This technique is a form of backstitch.

Adding Beads Over Knitted Stitches

To add beads over knitted stitches, each bead needs to be about the same size as one knitted stitch and the knitting needs to be firm. Pass over and under the knitted stitches rather than piercing them.

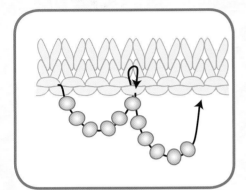

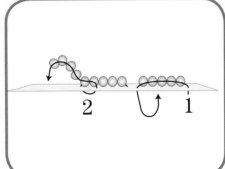

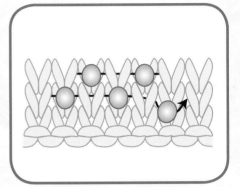

Begin with the thread coming out at the edge of the knitting. String a loop of beads. *Pass through the knitted edge enough stitches away to make the beads hang in a loop. Pass back through the last bead strung. String the same pattern of beads, less the first bead in the pattern, and repeat from asterisk.

Come up from the back of the knitting and string about 3–5 beads. *Pass back down through the knitting, making the stitch the length of the group of beads. Pass back up through the knitting 1–2 bead widths back from the end of the stitch (1), and pass through 1–2 of the beads. String another group of beads (2) and repeat from asterisk.

Come up from the back of the knitting to the right or left of the stitch to cover. String a bead, pass over the stitch to cover and then stitch back down to the back of the knitting, passing along the same row of knitting to the next stitch to cover with a bead.

Embroidery

One of the projects in this book (the *Sparkling Leaves Spring Hat* on page 52) utilizes what is known as the filled lazy daisy stitch, a type of embroidery stitch often used for petals and leaves.

These stitches are sewn through the knitting as if it is a piece of fabric. They can be worked in any size thread, from thin decorative embroidery threads to the yarn used to knit your project. Use a sharp needle, such as a chenille needle, when working these stitches. Where you embroider in this technique, you will eliminate the stretch in the knitting, so keep that in mind when planning your design.

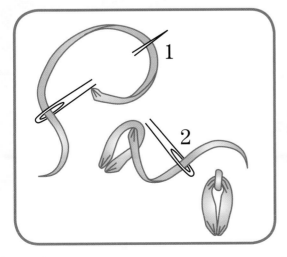

Bring the needle up through the fabric at your desired starting point. Insert the needle down into the fabric very close to the starting point. Bring the needle back up through the fabric at the end position of the stitch. Loop the yarn under the needle (1). Insert the needle down into the fabric on the other side of the yarn, forming a tiny stitch to hold the loop of yarn in place (2).

Chapter

2

Hats

Hats are naturally portable knits: They are often knit in one piece, require a small amount of yarn and are easy to make. For these reasons, we've decided to devote an entire chapter to them.

Each of the hats in this section has its own special characteristic. Some, like the *Berry Bramble Hat* (page 48) and the *Sparkling Leaves Spring Hat* (page 52) are embellished with beads, embroidery or buttons. Others, like the *Earflap Hat* (page 60), are cozy, unisex accessories that will keep out the winter chill and still look fabulous. The *Fedora Hat* (page 56) can be knit on the go and then fulled at home, making for a custom-fitted, stylish piece that also makes a great gift.

Stretchy I-Cord Hat

— Heidi Boyd

Need a perfect last-minute shower gift for the expectant mother in your life? This soft and stretchy hat will keep a baby's head warm for months to come. It's a great gift to make if you're pressed for time; just slip the yarn (which comes in supersmall and portable skeins) and two circular needles into your purse, and knit when you have the chance.

HAT

With CC, CO 70 (78, 92) sts. Divide evenly between the 2 circular needles (or DPNs) and join for working in the rnd, taking care not to twist sts.

Work in St st for 2 (3, 3)" [5 (8,8)cm]. Change to MC. Cont in St st until hat measures 5 (5½, 6½)" [13 (14, 17)cm] from cast-on edge, dec 1 st on last rnd for the 2 larger sizes—70 (77, 91) sts.

Next rnd: *K5, k2tog; rep from * to end—60 (66, 78) sts.

Knit 1 rnd.

Next rnd: *K4, k2tog; rep from * to end—50 (55, 65) sts.

Knit 1 rnd.

Next rnd: *K3, k2tog; rep from * to end—40 (44, 52) sts.

MORE ➧

Materials

SIZES

Newborn (6–12 mos, 12–24 mos)

FINISHED MEASUREMENTS

Hat circumference: 12 (13½, 16)" [30 (34, 41)cm], unstretched

YARN

1 skein each Cascade Yarns Fixation (cotton/elastic blend, 1.75oz/50g, 100yd/91m) in color #9349 Sunset (MC), color #9939 Desert Sand (CC)

NEEDLES

2 US size 9 (5.5mm) circular knitting needles

or 1 set of US size 9 (5.5mm) DPNs

NOTIONS

Tapestry needle

Stitch marker

GAUGE

23 sts and 34 rows = 4" (10cm) in St st

Knit 1 rnd.

Next rnd: *K2, k2tog; rep from * to end—30 (33, 39) sts.

Knit 1 rnd.

Next rnd: *K1, k2tog; rep from * to end—20 (22, 26) sts.

Knit 1 rnd.

Next rnd: K2tog around—10 (11, 13) sts.

Sizes Newborn and 6–12 mos only:

Next rnd: K0 (1), *k2tog; rep from * to end—5 (6) sts.

Size 12–24 mos only:

Next rnd: K1, *k3tog; rep from * to end—5 sts.

Work in I-cord on rem sts for 3" (8cm). (See page 33 in the *Getting Started* section for step-by-step instructions on knitting I-cord.) Break yarn, draw through sts and fasten off. Tie cord into an overhand knot, flush against top of hat. Weave in ends.

Take-Along Tip

Cascade Fixation is one adaptable yarn. Its elasticity allows it to be knitted in a huge range of needle sizes. When you're knitting, be sure not to pull the yarn too tightly or hold it too loosely— give it even tension to ensure the best results.

About Heidi Boyd

Heidi has been a knitter since she was five. She learned to knit before she could read and was self taught from diagrams. She has ten titles with North Light. *Craftcycle* is the newest and showcases felted wool projects. *Simply Beautiful Beading* has been an all-time best seller. Heidi has also contributed to *Better Homes and Gardens* books and publications for over fifteen years. Other publications include *FamilyFun*, Interweave's *Stitch* magazine, and *Crafts 'n Things*.

Heidi lives in Maine with her husband, three children and a lovable dog. Much of her day is spent caring for her brood. Keeping enough food in the house for her teenage sons (sixteen and thirteen) is a challenge. Lovely little miss Celia (three and a half) has let her recapture the joy of having a young child in the house.

Heidi supports herself solely on designing for publications, teaching and participating in craft fairs.

Berry Bramble Hat

— Cosette Cornelius-Bates

Thrifted buttons and embroidered branches give this practical hat a playful and feminine appearance. Knit it in thick-and-thin handspun yarn to play up the texture of the moss stitch, or use Aran-weight recycled sweater yarn for a more well-worn look. The results are so cozy and warm you might not even notice the cold.

EMBELLISHMENT SKILLS

- Outline stitch
- Single satin stitch
- Crochet chain edging

HAT

With circular needle, CO 96 (102, 108) sts. Join for working in the rnd, being careful not to twist sts. Place marker for beg of rnd, if desired.

Rnds 1–2: *K1, p1; rep from * to end.

Rnds 3–4: *P1, k1; rep from * to end.

Rep Rnds 1–4 once more.

Change to St st and work even until piece measures 4 (4, 4½)" 10 (10, 11)cm from cast-on edge.

Crown Decreases

When knitting on the circular needle becomes uncomfortable, switch to DPNs.

Next rnd: *K14 (15, 16), k2tog, pm; rep from * to end—90 (96, 102) sts.

MORE ➡

Materials

SIZES
Adult S (M, L)

FINISHED MEASUREMENTS
Circumference: 20 (21½, 23)" [51 (55, 58)cm]

Height: 7½ (8, 8¾)" [19 (20, 22)cm]

YARN
Approximately 120 (140, 160) yds [110 (128, 146)m] heavy worsted or Aran-weight 100% wool yarn

Small amount of 100% wool yarn for embellishment

Shown: 2-ply thick-and-thin hand-spun yarn, thrifted oddments

NEEDLES
16" (41cm) US size 7 (4.5mm) circular knitting needle

Set of US size 7 (4.5mm) DPNs

NOTIONS
Quilting pencil or chalk

Removable markers or safety pins

Stitch markers

Tapestry needle

Size G (4.5mm) or H (5mm) crochet hook

5 ½" (13mm) buttons

GAUGE
19 sts and 28 rows = 4" (10cm) in St st

Knit 1 rnd.

Next rnd: *Knit to 2 sts before marker, k2tog; rep from * to end—84 (90, 96) sts.

Rep last 2 rnds 13 (14, 15) times more—6 (6, 6) sts.

Cut yarn, leaving a 6" (15cm) tail. Use tapestry needle to thread tail through rem sts, pull tight and fasten off. Weave in ends.

Earflaps

Lay hat flat so that beg of round is at center back. Count 10 (11, 12) sts from center back to the right and mark with safety pin or removable marker (marker 1). Count 22 (22, 22) sts from marker 1 to the right and mark with safety pin or removable marker (marker 2). Count 32 (36, 40) sts from marker 2 to the right and mark with safety pin or removable marker (marker 3). Count 22 (22, 22) sts from marker 3 to the right and mark with safety pin or removable marker (marker 4). With RS facing, pick up and knit 22 (22, 22) sts from cast-on edge, beg at marker 1 and working toward marker 2.

Rows 1–2: *K1, p1; rep from * to end.

Rows 3–4: *P1, k1; rep from * to end.

Next row: Cont in est patt, work to last 3 sts, work 2 tog, work 1—21 (21, 21) sts.

Rep last row 13 times more—8 (8, 8) sts.

Bind off.

For second earflap, pick up and knit 22 (22, 22) sts from cast-on edge, beg at marker 3 and working toward marker 4. Rep from ** to complete second earflap. Weave in ends.

Embellish

Using wool yarn, work a crochet chain edging around the bottom edge of the hat and earflaps. Transfer the embellishment pattern on page 51 to the knitted fabric with a quilting pencil or chalk. Using wool yarn and a tapestry needle, stitch the embroidery pattern using outline stitch starting at the bottom edge of the left earflap. (See photo for guidance in placement.) Following pattern, sew on buttons.

About Cosette Cornelius-Bates

Cosette Cornelius-Bates spends her time knitting, spinning, dyeing, teaching and designing in Pittsburgh, Pennsylvania. She became interested in wool while studying for a master's in Christian Studies in Theology and the Arts and ended up knitting her final arts project. Cosette can always be found in the virtual world on her Web site http://cosymakes. com and at her Etsy shop http://cosymakes. etsy.com. In the real world she can be found hawking her wares at craft fairs and yarn shows and stalking farmers at fiber festivals to see if she can acquire some of their wool. Her knitting patterns are collected in the book *Knit One, Embellish Too: Hats, Mittens and Scarves with a Twist*. She also has a line of independent knitting patterns available in her shop, along with her yarns.

Actual size

Sparkling Leaves Spring Hat

— Jane Davis

Dreaming of spring but stuck in dreary winter? With its easy construction and lovely leaf and flower embellishments, the *Sparkling Leaves Spring Hat* may be just what you're looking for. Knit the hat while you're out and about, but leave the beading and embroidery for when you're at home and can devote your full attention.

EMBELLISHMENT SKILLS

- Sewing beads
- Lazy daisy stitch

Materials

SIZES
One size

FINISHED MEASUREMENTS
Circumference: 22" (56cm)

YARN
1 ball Louisa Harding Impression (nylon/mohair blend, 1.75oz/50g, 154yd/141m), color #4 Emerald, Green, Yellow

1 ball Louisa Harding Kimono (angora/wool/nylon blend, .9oz/25g, 124yd/113m) color #8 Navy, Brown

1 ball Louisa Harding Fauve (100% nylon, 1.75oz/50g, 127yd/116m) color #6 Grass

1 ball Louisa Harding Sari Ribbon (nylon/metallic blend, 1.75oz./50g, 66yd/60m) color #2 Mint, Sky

NEEDLES
24" (61cm) US size 10½ (6.5mm) circular knitting needle

NOTIONS
Tapestry needle

1" (3cm) accent bead

4g size-8 mint-green seed beads

8 size-5 green seed beads

8 side-drilled oblong pale green pearls

Beading needle and beading thread to match yarn or beads

GAUGE
14 sts and 19 rows = 4" (10cm) in St st with three yarns held tog

HAT

Holding 3 of the different yarns together as one, not including the ribbon yarn, CO 72 sts.

Row 1: Knit.

Row 2: Purl.

Rows 3–4: (K1, p1) rep across.

Rows 5–6: (P1, k1) rep across.

Row 7: Knit.

MORE ➜

Row 8: Purl.

Rows 9–24: Continue in Stockinette stitch.

Row 25: (K2tog, k7) rep 8 times—64 sts.

Row 27: (K2tog, k6) rep 8 times—56 sts.

Row 29: (K2tog, k5) repeat 8 times—48 sts.

Continue in dec pattern until there are 16 sts left. Cut yarn to 18" (46cm), thread with tapestry needle, pass through remaining sts and sew seam closed using mattress stitch. Weave in ends. No need to block.

Embellish

Using the beading thread and needle, sew the accent bead to the hat approx 2" (5cm) from the bottom edge and about 3" (8cm) to the right of center. Using the thick ribbon and tapestry needle, stitch lazy daisy stitches radiating out from the accent bead (see page 41).

Stitch straight stitches of beads radiating out from the accent bead, stringing several size-8 beads, 1 pearl, 1 size-5 bead and 3 size-8 bead. Stitch several dangles below and to the side of the accent bead as shown below. Weave in ends.

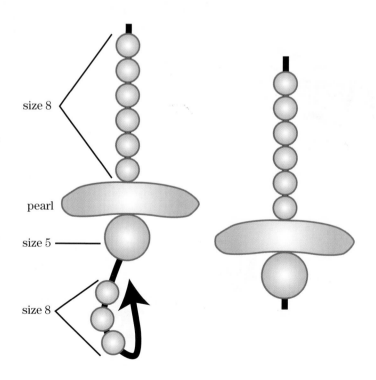

size 8

pearl

size 5

size 8

About Jane Davis

Jane Davis has an eclectic interest in beads, fiber, drawing and painting that has spanned over thirty years. She is a widely published author and designer who has written over a dozen arts-and-crafts books including *The Complete Guide to Beading Techniques* (Krause, 2001), *Felted Crochet* and *Bead Embroidery The Complete Guide* (Krause, 2005) and *Knitting The Complete Guide* (Krause, 2008). She has designed knitwear for yarn companies, including Classic Elite Yarns and Brown Sheep Company, and her work has been featured in magazines including *Vogue Knitting*, *Knitter's* and *Beadwork*. Jane has also appeared on cable and public television programs. She loves pattern, design and color and is always inspired by the luscious textures and colors of yarns in her favorite yarn store, Anacapa Fine Yarns in Ventura, California.

Fedora Hat

— *Jane Davis*

Making a fulled hat is exciting when you find out you can make it look just like a professionally made hat. One tip for making this hat is to take the time to full the fabric completely. But the real secret is to use a hat form and water-based shellac to get the finished hat to be the same shape and stiffness as a hat you would buy at a hat store.

HAT

Crown

With DPNs, CO 6 sts and join for working in the rnd.

Rnd 1: Knit all sts.

Rnd 2: *Kfb; rep from * to end—12 sts.

Rnd 3: Knit all sts.

Rnd 4: *Pm, kfb, k1; rep from * to end—18 sts, 6 markers.

Rnd 5: Knit all sts.

Rnd 6: *Sm, kfb, k2; rep from * to end—24 sts.

Rnd 7: Knit all sts.

Rnd 8: *Sm, kfb, k to next m; rep from * to end—30 sts.

Rep Rnds 7–8 10 times more—90 sts.

MORE ➡

Materials

SIZES
One size

FINISHED MEASUREMENTS
Crown circumference: 22" (56cm)

Brim circumference: 34" (86cm)

YARN
1 skein Harrisville Designs New England Highland (100% wool, 3.5oz/100g, 200yd/183m), color #39 Russet

NEEDLES
24" (61cm) US size 9 (5.5mm) circular knitting needle

Set of US size 9 (5.5mm) DPNs

NOTIONS
Stitch marker

Tapestry needle

Grosgrain ribbon

Double-fold bias binding

Stabilizer

Small feathers (optional)

White craft glue (optional)

FULLING SUPPLIES
Hot, soapy water

Hat form

Steam iron

Wooden mallet

Water-based shellac

GAUGE
16 sts and 22 rows = 4" (10cm) in St st, before fulling

Narrow Brim

Work 25 rnds even.

Next rnd: *Sm, kfb, k to next m; rep from * to end—96 sts.

Next rnd: Knit all sts.

Rep last 2 rnds 6 times more—132 sts.

BO. Weave in ends.

Wide Brim Variation

Work 35 rnds even.

Next rnd: *Sm, kfb, k to next m; rep from * to end—96 sts.

Next rnd: Knit all sts.

Rep last 2 rnds 9 times more—150 sts.

BO. Weave in ends.

Fulling

Hand-full the hat in a sinkful of hot, soapy water until it begins to shrink (see *Fulling Knitted and Crocheted Fabric*, page 38). Check the hat on the hat form occasionally for size and continue fulling until the hat fits snugly on the form. Rinse out the soap with warm water and squeeze as much water out of the hat as possible. Using the steam iron, heat the hat and then shape it on the hat form, pounding the surface with a wooden mallet to get a smooth, tight-fitting shape. Let the hat dry on the form. When the hat is completely dry, apply the water-based shellac following the manufacturer's instructions.

Assembly

Pin a strip of stabilizer to the inside edge of the hat just above the brim and adjust it so the hat is the desired size; trim the ends so they overlap approximately ½"

(1cm). Stitch the stabilizer to the bottom edge of the hat, along the fold. Cover the stabilizer with double-fold bias binding and sew in place. Cut a 22" (56cm) strip of grosgrain ribbon and steam press it so one edge is longer than the other, creating a gentle curve. Place the ribbon on the outside of the hat and adjust it until it fits snugly around the brim of the hat, with the raw edges meeting on the left side of the hat. Pin the ribbon in place. If desired, create a bow with an additional piece of ribbon. Pin the bow over the raw edges of the ribbon on the brim of the hat. Adjust the ribbons so they are even and snug and the raw edges of the ribbon are covered by the bow. Sew the ribbon in place along the brim of the hat and tack the bow edges in place. If desired, slide one or more feathers behind the bow. If they don't fit snuggly, use a small amount of glue to adhere them behind the bow.

Earflap Hat

— *Hannah Fettig*

This hat is made out of The Fibre Company's Pemaquid, a soft, warm yarn with a beautiful shine. An incredibly fast project, the finished hat is so hip your friends will all want one, too. As a finishing touch, the hat features fun cable ties.

HAT

With size US 10 (6.0mm) circular needle and MC, CO 70 sts.

Join for working in the rnd, taking care not to twist sts.

Work in St st for 3½" (9cm)—70 sts.

Dec rnd 1: * K8, k2tog; rep from * to end of rnd—63 sts.

Knit 1 rnd.

Dec rnd 2: * K7, k2tog; rep from * to end of rnd—56 sts.

Knit 1 rnd.

Dec rnd 3: * K6, k2tog; rep from * to end of rnd—49 sts.

Knit 1 rnd.

Dec rnd 4: * K5, k2tog; rep from * to end of rnd—42 sts.

MORE➤

Materials

SIZES
One size

FINISHED MEASUREMENTS
Circumference: 17" (43cm) unstretched

Height: 7¾" (20cm)

Cabled ties: 19" (48cm)

YARN
1 skein each of The Fibre Company Pemaquid (alpaca/merino/soy silk blend, 1.75oz/50 g, 60yd/55m) in color Cranberry (MC) and color Granite (CC)

NEEDLES
16" (41cm) US size 9 (5.5mm) circular knitting needle

16" (41cm) US size 10 (6.0mm) circular knitting needle

Set of US size 10 (6.0mm) DPNs

NOTIONS
Tapestry needle

Stitch markers

Stitch holder

Cable needle

GAUGE
16 sts and 24 rows = 4" (10cm) in St st with larger needle

Knit 1 rnd.

Note: When necessary, switch to size US 10 (6.0mm) DPNs.

Dec rnd 5: * K4, k2tog; rep from * to end of rnd—35 sts.

Knit 1 rnd.

Dec rnd 6: * K3, k2tog; rep from * to end of rnd—28 sts.

Knit 1 rnd.

Dec rnd 7: * K2, k2tog; rep from * to end of rnd—21 sts.

Knit 1 rnd.

Dec rnd 8: * K1, k2tog; rep from * to end of rnd—14 sts.

Knit 1 rnd.

Dec Rnd 9: * K2tog; rep from * to end of rnd—7 sts.

Break yarn, pull tight through rem sts.

With MC and size US 9 (5.5mm) 16" (41cm) circular needle, with RS facing, pick up and knit 70 sts along bottom edge of hat. Pm to mark beg of rnd. Work in k1, p1 rib for 2" (5cm).

Next rnd: BO 10 sts, work 15 sts in patt, place these 15 sts on a holder, BO 20 sts, work 15 sts in patt, place these 15 sts on a holder, BO rem 10 sts.

Earflaps (make 2)

Place 15 earflap sts on size US 9 (5.5mm) needle. Cont working with MC.

Row 1 (RS): P1, k1, p1, k9, p1, k1, p1—15 sts.

Row 2: K1, p1, k1, p9, k1, p1, k1.

About Hannah Fettig

Hannah Fettig is a knitwear designer living in Portland, Maine. She is the author of *Closely Knit: Handmade Gifts for the Ones You Love*. Her designs have also been featured in *Interweave Knits*. Original patterns are available for purchase from her Web site, www.knitbot.com.

Begin Cabled Ties (make 2)

Row 3: P1, k2tog, slide 3 sts onto cn, hold in back, k1, k3 from cn, k1, slide 1 st onto cn, hold in front, k3, k1 from cn, k2tog, p1—13 sts.

Row 4: K1, p11, k1.

Row 5: P1, k2tog, k7, k2tog, p1—11 sts.

Row 6: K1, p9, k1.

Row 7: P1, slide 3 sts onto cn, hold in back, k1, k3 from cn, k1, slide 1 st onto cn, hold in front, k3, k1 from cn, p1.

Row 8: K1, p9, k1.

Row 9: P1, k9, p1.

Rows 10–11: Rep Rows 6–7.

Row 12: P2tog, purl to last 2 sts, p2tog—9 sts.

Switch to CC.

Work foll 4 rows of cable pattern 28 times, or until tie is desired length:

Row 1: K9.

Row 2: P9.

Row 3: Slide 3 sts onto cn, hold in back, k1, k3 from cn, k1, slide 1 st onto cn, hold in front, k3, k1 from cn—9 sts.

Row 4: P9.

BO 9 sts.

Finishing
Weave in all ends.

Hat and Soul

— Jonelle Raffino and Prudence Mapstone

This hat looks like it would be difficult to master, but that intricate lace is just random chain stitching. Deceptively simple yet excitingly beautiful, *Hat and Soul* will add a touch of whimsy and glamour to your winter accessories.

HAT

Using yarn A, CO 72 sts. Work in St st for 30" (76cm). Bind off.

Felting

Felt until piece measures approximately 12" × 25" (30cm × 64cm). Lay flat and allow to dry completely.

Assembly

Enlarge the template on page 67 and trace the appropriate outline onto a piece of heavy paper or cardboard. Use the pattern to cut 5 identical panels from the felted rectangle.

MORE ➡

Materials

SIZES

Women's medium

FINISHED MEASUREMENTS

Head circumference: 22½" (57cm) after felting

YARN

1 skein SWTC Karaoke (SOYSILK® /wool blend, 1.75oz/50g, 109yd/100m) (A)

1 skein SWTC TOFUtsies (superwash wool/SOYSILK® /cotton/chitin blend, 3.5oz/100g, 464yd/424m) (B)

NEEDLES AND HOOKS

US size 7 (4.5mm) straight knitting needles
Size B (2.25mm) crochet hook

NOTIONS

Heavy paper or cardboard
Tapestry needle

GAUGE

20 sts = 4" (10cm) in pattern using yarn A (before felting)

Base Round

Using a crochet hook and yarn B, work a rnd of [sc, ch 1] evenly spaced around the edge of each piece. Fasten off.

Holding 2 hat panels with WS tog, use yarn B to work a row of sc sts into the edging, working through sts on both panels at once to seam them tog. Both the sc and the ch-1 sp in the previous rnd count as sts when joining. Adjust as needed to keep fabric smooth and free from puckers. Cont as est with rem panels. Weave in ends.

Freeform Embellishments

Rejoin yarn B at lower corner of first panel. Ch desired number of sts and join close to beg of ch to make a loop on the surface of the panel. Cont working over the surface of the piece, randomly making ch sts and connecting them either to edging sts or previous ch to make a lacy freeform mesh all over the surface of the felted panel. Keep an eye on how things are progressing as you add each new section of crochet to ensure the desired result. Rep on rem panels. Weave in ends.

About Prudence Mapstone

Prudence has been a knitter ever since she was about seven years old, when her mother taught her the basics. As a teen she figured out how to crochet after buying a hook and just messing around. Learning the actual names of the stitches came years later, when she was invited to conduct workshops after she exhibited some of her freeform artworks and discovered that there was an interest in the way she combined knitting with crochet in a freeform manner.

You can see many examples of her art-to-wear garments at www.knotjustknitting.com. Recently, she has also been keeping a blog entitled *A Scrumble a Week* at http://prudencemapstone.blogspot.com.

For many years Prudence has been teaching her methods around the world, and she has self-published a number of books including *Freeform: Serendipitous Design Techniques for Knitting and Crochet.* Her most recent book, *Freeform Style,* coauthored with Jonelle Raffino, was published by North Light in 2009. Her designs always encourage many different color, placement and/or stitch options, enabling the knitter to stamp each item with their own personality.

Prudence lives in Brisbane, Australia. Now an empty nester, she shares her home with her husband of thirty-eight years . . . and an enormous yarn stash.

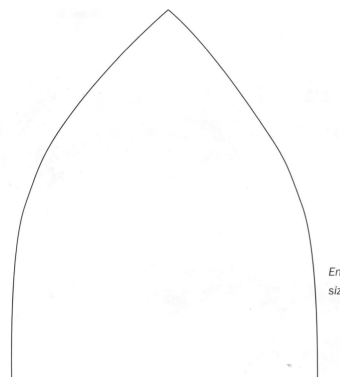

Enlarge template by 143 percent to bring to full size. Use this template for each of the panels.

About Jonelle Raffino

Jonelle Raffino is the creative force behind SWTC Inc., the yarn company that pioneered earth-friendly fibers like SOYSILK®, bamboo, and corn fiber for handknitting. She is also the author of *Socks à la Carte* and *Purls Forever*. To see more of Jonelle's work and learn about SWTC, visit www.soysilk.com.

Chapter 3

Scarves and Gloves

Winter is fast approaching: The snow has begun to fall, the air is freezing and the sky is gray. What's a busy knitter to do? Try taking along a series of chill-proof knitting projects that will keep you and your family and friends toasty and warm, even in the midst of snowball fights and sledding.

The scarves and gloves in this section are as practical and warm as they are beautiful and stylish. Drape yourself in luxury with the *Cashmere Ruffles Scarf* (page 76) and the *Lacy Accent Scarf* (page 78) or use up scrap yarn from your stash by knitting the *Sideways Scarf* (page 80). If your fingers are aching from the cold, perhaps the best remedy is a pair of gloves or mittens: The *Cabled Gloves* (page 82) are all about intricate stitches and crocheted accents, while the *Snow Day Mittens* (page 70) are a simple, fun project that calls for just a tiny bit of embroidery. These projects knit up fast and make great gifts; the recipients will surely think of you the next time they bundle up in their handmade scarves and gloves!

Snow Day Mittens

— Cosette Cornelius-Bates

What's better than a snow day spent sledding or making snow angels? Worked with worsted weight yarn and smaller needles, these mittens will keep your hands dry and shiver-free. The snowflakes add a fun touch, and the bright color will keep dropped mittens from being lost in the snow.

EMBELLISHMENT SKILLS

- Single satin stitch

Materials

SIZES

Child M (L, XL)

6–18 mos. (4–6 years, 6–8 years)

FINISHED MEASUREMENTS

Palm circumference: 5½ (6, 6½)" [14 (15, 17)cm]

Length: 6¼ (6¾, 7¼)" [16 (17, 18)cm]

YARN

Approximately 80 (90, 100) yds [73 (82, 91)m] worsted weight 100% wool yarn

Small amount of 100% wool yarn for embellishment

Shown: recycled sweater yarn, thrifted oddments

NEEDLES

Set of US size 4 (3.5mm) DPNs

NOTIONS

Scrap yarn

Stitch marker

Tapestry needle

GAUGE

24 sts and 36 rows = 4" (10cm) in St st

MITTENS (MAKE 2)

CO 32 (36, 40) sts. Divide as evenly as possible over 3 DPNs and join for working in the rnd, being careful not to twist sts.

Rnd 1: *K1, p1; rep from * to end.

Rep Rnd 1 until piece measures 2 (2¼, 2¼)" [5 (6, 6)cm] from cast-on edge. Change to St st and knit 2 rnds.

Thumb Gusset

Next rnd: K15 (17, 19), pm, M1L, K1, M1R, pm, knit to end—34 (38, 42) sts; 3 sts between markers.

Knit 1 rnd.

Next rnd: Knit to marker, sm, M1L, knit to marker, M1R, sm, knit to end—36 (40, 44) sts; 5 sts between markers.

MORE➡

71

Rep last 2 rnds 3 (4, 5) times—42 (48, 54) sts; 11 (13, 15) sts between markers.

Knit 1 rnd.

Next rnd: Knit to marker, remove marker, slip next 11 (13, 15) sts onto scrap yarn. Remove second marker, CO 1 st over gap. (See page 19 for instructions on casting on backward-loop style.) Knit rem sts—32 (36, 40)sts.

Work even until piece measures 3¼ (3½, 4)" [8 (9, 10)cm] from top of cuff or until mitten reaches to tip of pinky finger.

Top Decreases

Redistribute sts over needles—11 (12, 13) sts on first needle, 11 (12, 13) sts on second needle, 10 (12, 14) sts on third needle.

Dec rnd: *Knit to last 2 sts on needle, k2tog; rep from * to end—29 (33, 37) sts.

Knit 1 rnd.

Rep last 2 rnds twice more—23 (27, 31) sts.

Rep Dec Rnd only 6 (7, 8) times more—5 (6, 7) sts.

Cut yarn, leaving a 6" (15cm) tail. Use tapestry needle to thread tail through rem sts, pull tight and fasten off.

Thumb

Place 11 (13, 15) sts from scrap yarn onto DPNs. Knit 1 rnd, picking up and knitting 1 st over gap—12 (14, 16) sts. Work even in St st for ¾ (1, 1¼)" [2 (3, 3)cm].

Next rnd: *K2, k2tog; rep from * to end, end with k2tog for size M—9 (10, 12) sts.

Knit 1 rnd.

Next rnd: K1 (0, 0), *k2tog; rep from * to end—5 (5, 6) sts.

Cut yarn, leaving a 6" (15cm) tail. Use tapestry needle to thread tail through rem sts, pull tight and fasten off. Weave in ends. If there are any holes where the thumb meets the hand, use your yarn tail to close them.

Embellish

Randomly embroider eight-pointed stars over the mittens using single satin stitch.

Silky Smoke Ring

— *Cosette Cornelius-Bates*

Smoke rings are a versatile and practical garment, and this version is knitted in a solid fabric for added warmth. Wear it over your head to cover your ears without messing up your hair, or pin on a clip-on earring or old brooch and wear it as a cowl. Best of all, this project requires only one skein of yarn and one circular needle, so bringing it along is a breeze!

SMOKE RING

CO 100 sts. Join for working in the rnd, being careful not to twist sts. Place marker for beg of rnd, if desired.

Border
*Purl 1 rnd. Knit 1 rnd. Rep from * once more.

Knit 2 rnds.

Next rnd: *K1, p1; rep from * to end.

Pattern
Rnds 1–3: Knit.

Rnd 4: *K3, p1; rep from * to end.

Rnds 5–7: Knit.

Rnd 8: K1, *p1, k3; rep from * to last 3 sts, p1, k2.

Rep Rnds 1–8 7 times more, then Rnds 1–7 once more.

Border
Purl 1 rnd. Knit 1 rnd. Purl 1 rnd.

Finishing
BO all sts. Weave in ends.

Embellish
Attach a clip-on earring or brooch to the knitted fabric.

Materials

SIZES
One size

FINISHED MEASUREMENTS
Circumference: 22" (56cm)

Height: 13½" (34cm)

YARN
1 skein Cascade Success (alpaca/silk blend, 1.75oz/50g, 210yd/192m)

NEEDLES
16" (40cm) US size 9 (5.5mm) circular knitting needle

NOTIONS
Stitch marker

Tapestry needle

Clip-on earring or brooch

GAUGE
18 sts and 24 rows = 4" (10cm) in St st

Cashmere Ruffles Scarf

— Hannah Fettig

If you haven't knitted with cashmere before, you're in for a treat. This luxurious fiber, known for its softness and gorgeous sheen, is suited for projects that will be worn close to the skin. The *Cashmere Ruffles Scarf* is great for long car trips or plane rides during which you can concentrate on the short row shaping.

Materials

SIZES
One size

FINISHED MEASUREMENTS
Approximately 8" × 51" (20cm × 130cm)

YARN
4 skeins Karabella Yarns Boise (cashmere/merino wool blend, 1.75oz/50g, 163yd/149m) color #63 Wine Red

NEEDLES
US size 5 (3.75mm) straight knitting needles

NOTIONS
Tapestry needle

GAUGE
24 sts and 32 rows = 4" (10cm) in St st

Short Row Shaping

(RS) Wrap and Turn (W&T): Wyif, sl 1 st from the left needle to the right. Move the yarn to the back, sl st back to the left needle, turn work. 1 st has been wrapped.

(WS) Wrap and Turn (W&T): Wyib, sl 1 st from the left needle to the right. Move the yarn to the front, sl st back to the left needle, turn work. 1 st has been wrapped.

Note

Whenever you come to a wrap, work the wrap tog with the st it wraps. To pick up a wrap and its st, slide the tip of the right needle into the wrap from the front of the work and place the wrap on the left needle alongside the st it wraps. Knit the 2 loops tog as one st.

SCARF

With size US 5 (3.75mm) needles, CO 55 sts.

Purl 1 row.

Knit 1 row.

Begin Pattern Stitch

Row 1 (RS): K22, w&t.

Row 2: P22.

Row 3: K24, w&t.

Row 4: P24.

Rows 5–6: Rep Rows 1–2.

Row 7: K25, p5, k25.

Row 8 (WS): P22, w&t.

Row 9: K22.

Row 10: P24, w&t.

Row 11: K24.

Rows 12–13: Rep Rows 8–9.

Row 14: P25, k5, p25.

Row 15 (RS): Purl.

Row 16: Knit.

Rep Rows 1–16 of pattern stitch until scarf reaches desired length.

BO all sts. Weave in ends.

Lacy Accent Scarf

— Stefanie Japel

Feel glamorous in no time with this fast-knitting, classy scarf. The lace pattern is easy to memorize, and in a smooth wool/silk blend, you'll be amazed at how quickly it knits up. Experiment with different yarns and weights—it will look equally fabulous in a bulky or worsted weight yarn.

LACE PATTERN

Work lace patt over a multiple of 7 sts +1.

Row 1: K1, *p1, k1, yo, p2tog, k1, p1, k1; rep from * to end.

Row 2: P1, *k2, yo, p2tog, k2, p1; rep from * to end.

Rep Rows 1–2.

SCARF

Cast on 50 sts. Work in lace patt until piece measures 72" (183cm). Bind off.

Finishing

Weave in ends. Block lightly.

Materials

SIZES
One size

FINISHED MEASUREMENTS
6½" × 72" (17cm × 183cm)

YARN
1 ball JaggerSpun Zephyr Wool-Silk 2/18 (merino wool/Chinese tussah silk blend, 2oz/57g, 630 yd/566m), color Teal

NEEDLES
US size 6 (4.0mm) straight knitting needles

NOTIONS
Tapestry needle

GAUGE
31 sts and 20 rows = 4" (10cm) in lace pattern

About Stefanie Japel

Stefanie learned to knit from her grandma when she was eight years old. She grew up wearing her sweaters and borrowing the ones she made for other people. Most of these sweaters were raglans, knit in the round from the top. She continues this sweater-making tradition.

Stefanie has written two books: *Fitted Knits* and *Glam Knits*. Her work has appeared in a number of books and publications including *Big Girl Knits, Stitch 'N Bitch Nation, Knitgrrl, Knit Wit, Not Another Teen Knitting Book, Interweave Knits, Knitscene, Knit.1,* and *Vogue Knitting.* She has designed patterns for Stitch Diva Studios and the yarn companies Southwest Trading Company, JCA Reynolds, Artful Yarns, Tilli Tomas and Mission Falls.

Stefanie is married and has one cat and one daughter.

Sideways Scarf

— *Libby Bruce*

This scarf is the perfect companion to a chilly autumn evening and a cup of warm cider. Knit lengthwise in a multitude of colors, it can be muted or wild depending on the shades you choose. The pattern allows any mistakes you make to look intentional, so you don't necessarily have to devote your full attention to the project at hand. You can knit and chat to your heart's content.

SCARF

CO 240 sts, pm at 120 sts (center).

Rows 1–4: With A, knit.

Row 5: With B, purl.

Row 6: With B, knit.

Row 7: With B, purl.

Row 8: With B, knit to marker, purl to end.

Rows 9–10: With C, knit to marker, purl to end.

Rows 11–14: With C, knit.

Row 15: With A, purl.

Rows 16–18: With A, purl to marker, knit to end.

Rows 18–21: With D, knit.

Rep Rows 1–21 once more. Bind off.

Finishing

Weave in ends.

About Libby Bruce

Libby Bruce became ruthlessly addicted to knitting in college. Today she knits in Columbus, Ohio, where she lives with her awesome husband and two ill-behaved cats. She blogs about knitting and yarn at http://winelips.blogspot.com and teaches knitting classes through her business, WonderKnit.

In addition to knitting, Libby loves books, animals, trouble, rock and roll and things topped with melted cheese. One day she hopes to run the nicest alpaca farm in town.

Materials

SIZES
One size

FINISHED MEASUREMENTS
6" × 60" (15cm × 152cm)

YARN
2 skeins each Karabella Aurora 8 (100% wool, 1.75oz/50g, 98yd/90m) color #910 Purple (A) and color #716 Parsley (B)

1 skein each Karabella Aurora 8 color #190 Blue (C) and color #49 Brown (D)

NEEDLES
40" (102cm) US size 7 (4.5mm) circular knitting needle

NOTIONS
Stitch marker

Tapestry needle

GAUGE
16 sts = 4" (10cm) in garter st

Cabled Gloves

— Jonelle Raffino and Prudence Mapstone

Bundle up in style with these beautifully detailed gloves that combine knitting and crochet stitches to create a truly unique accessory. Freeform crochet is a special technique that can be developed with practice and a healthy dose of creativity. Use this pattern as a starting point for adding crochet embellishments to other projects.

GLOVES

Lace Pattern Stitch

Rnds 1–2: *P2, k3; rep from * to last 2 sts, p2.

Rnd 3: *P2, slip 3rd knit st on left needle over other 2 knit sts and then knit those 2 sts; rep from * to last 2 sts, p2.

Rnd 4: *P2, k1, yo, k1; rep from * to last 2 sts, p2.

Rep Rnds 1–4 for pattern.

Note: The glove pattern begins at the top of the wrist, and the cuff is added with freeform embellishment after the knitting is complete.

Lower Hand (Both Gloves)

With yarn A, CO 43 sts. Join, being careful not to twist sts. Knit 1 rnd.

Work lace patt over 22 sts for back of hand. Work rem 21 sts in St st for palm. Work even as est for 12 rnds.

Thumb Gusset (Right Hand)

Rnd 1: Work Row 1 of lace patt to last 2 purl sts, pm, p1, M1, p1, pm, work St st to end of rnd.

Cont in lace patt and St st as est, inc as foll between markers for Thumb Gusset:

Rnd 2: M1, k3, M1.

MORE ➤

Materials

SIZES

One size

FINISHED MEASUREMENTS

Hand circumference: 7" (18cm) at widest part of hand

YARN

2 skeins SWTC Yin (wool/silk/bamboo blend, 1.75oz/50g, 167yd/153m) (A)

1 skein SWTC Yin in 2 to 4 additional colors, as desired, for the freeform embellishment

NEEDLES AND HOOKS

Set of US size 5 (3.75mm) DPNs

Size F (3.75mm) crochet hook

NOTIONS

2 stitch markers

4 small stitch holders

Tapestry needle

GAUGE

24 sts and 28 rows = 4" (10cm) in St st

Rnd 3: M1, p1, pass 3rd knit st over 2 sts and then knit those 2 sts, p1, M1.

Rnd 4: P2, k1, yo, k1, p2.

Rnd 5: M1, p2, k3, p2, M1.

Rnd 6: P3, k3, p2, k1.

Rnd 7: M1, p3, pass 3rd knit st over 2 sts, then knit those 2 sts, p2, k1, M1.

Rnd 8: P4, k1, yo, k1, p2, k2.

Rnd 9: M1, p1, k1, p2, k3, p2, k2, M1.

Rnd 10: P2, k1, p2, k3, p2, k3.

Rnd 11: M1, p1, k2, p2, pass 3rd st over 2 sts and knit those 2 sts, p2, k3, M1.

Rnd 12: P2, k2, p2, k1, yo, k1, p2, k4—15 gusset sts between markers.

Cont in patt without inc until gusset measures 2¾" (7cm).

Work across back of hand sts, place Thumb Gusset sts on 2 holders, CO 2 sts to bridge gap, knit across palm sts—43 hand sts.

Cont in patt, purling over the 2 cast-on sts, working until hand measures 3½" (9cm) from start of Thumb Gusset.

Little Finger

Keeping in patt as est, work across 6 sts, place next 33 sts on 2 holders, CO 2 sts to bridge gap, k4—12 sts.

Next rnd: Work in rnd on these sts in est patt (p1, k1) over cast-on sts until Little Finger measures 2¼" (6cm).

Next rnd: K2tog across—6 sts.

Cut yarn and run tail through rem sts to close. Weave in tail.

Upper Hand

Reattach yarn at base of Little Finger on back of hand, work in patt across back of hand, knit palm sts, pick up 2 sts at base of Little Finger—35 sts.

Knit 1 more rnd in patt (k1, p1 over picked-up sts).

Ring Finger

Work over next 5 sts, place next 23 sts on 2 holders, CO 2 sts to bridge gap, work across rem 7 sts—14 sts.

Work in patt (p1, k1 over cast-on sts) until finger measures 2½" (6cm). Complete as for Little Finger.

Middle Finger

Reattach yarn at base of Ring Finger on back of hand. Work across 5 sts, place 13 sts on holder, CO 2 sts to bridge gap, work across rem 5 sts, pick up 2 sts at base of Ring Finger—14 sts.

Keep in patt (p1, k1 over cast-on sts and k1, p1 over picked-up sts), work until finger measures 3" (8cm). Complete as for Little Finger.

Index Finger

Reattach yarn at base of Middle Finger on back of hand. Work across 13 sts, pick up 2 sts at base of Middle Finger—15 sts.

Keeping in patt (k1, p1 over picked-up sts) work until finger measures 2¾" (7cm). Complete as for Little Finger, working k1 at end of last rnd.

Thumb

Reattach yarn at base of Thumb on back of hand. Work 15 sts, pick up 2 sts at base of thumb opening—17 sts.

Maintain lace patt up Thumb (p2, k3, p2 section) while keeping rem sts in St st. Work until Thumb measures 2" (5cm).

Next rnd: K2tog around, end k1—9 sts.

Next rnd: K2tog around, end k1—5 sts.

Cut yarn and thread through rem sts to close. Weave in ends.

Thumb Gusset (Left Glove)

Work Lower Hand as for right glove.

Rnd 1: Pm, p1, M1, p1, pm. Cont in lace patt for back of hand and St st for palm.

Inc between markers as foll for Thumb Gusset:

Rnd 2: M1, k3, M1.

Rnd 3: M1, p1, slip 3rd st over 2 sts and then knit those 2 sts, p1, M1.

Rnd 4: P2, k1, yo, k1, p2.

Rnd 5: M1, p2, k3, p2, M1.

Rnd 6: K1, p2, k3, p3.

Rnd 7: M1, k1, p2, slip 3rd st over 2 sts and then knit those 2 sts, p4, M1.

Rnd 8: K2, p2, k1, yo, k1, p4.

Rnd 9: M1, k3, p2, k3, p2, k1, p1, M1.

Rnd 10: K3, p2, k3, p2, k1, p2.

Rnd 11: M1, k3, p2, slip 3rd st over 2 sts and then knit those 2 sts, p2, k2, p1, M1.

Rnd 12: K4, p2, k1, yo, k1, p2, k2, p2—15 gusset sts between markers.

Cont in patt without inc until gusset measures 2¾" (7cm).

Work across palm sts, place Thumb Gusset sts on 2 holders, CO 2 sts to bridge gap, work across back sts—43 hand sts.

Keeping in patt and purling over the 2 cast-on sts, work until hand measures 3½" (9cm) from start of Thumb Gusset.

Little Finger

Work across 4 sts, place next 33 sts on 2 holders, CO 2 sts to bridge gap, work across rem 6 sts—12 sts.

Keeping in patt (k1, p1 over cast-on sts), complete as for Right Glove Little Finger.

Upper Hand

Reattach yarn at base of Little Finger on palm side. Work 1 rnd in patt, pick up 2 sts at base of Little Finger. Complete 1 more rnd (p1, k1 over picked-up sts).

Ring Finger

Work over next 7 sts, place 23 sts on holders. CO 2 sts to bridge gap, work across rem 5 sts—14 sts.

Keeping in patt (k1, p1 over cast-on sts), complete as for Right Glove.

Middle Finger

Reattach yarn at base of Ring Finger on palm side. Work across 5 sts, place 13 sts on holder, CO 2 sts to bridge gap, work across rem 5 sts, pick up 2 sts at base of Ring Finger—14 sts.

Keeping in patt (k1, p1 over cast-on sts and p1, k1 over picked-up sts), complete as for Right Glove.

Index Finger

Reattach yarn at base of Middle Finger on palm side. Work across 13 sts, pick up 2 sts at base of Middle Finger—15 sts.

Keeping in patt (p1, k1 over picked-up sts), complete as for Right Glove.

Thumb

Reattach yarn at base of Thumb on palm side. Work across 15 sts, pick up 2 sts at base of thumb opening—17 sts.

Complete as for Right Glove.

Finishing

Weave in ends.

FREEFORM CUFF

Crochet Domes (make 25–30)

With crochet hook and desired color, ch 3 and join with a sl st to form a ring. Ch 3 again and work 6 dc into the ring. Join with a sl st to the top of ch 3 to close. Fasten off.

Assembly

Arrange domes to create a cuff on each glove, making the cuffs as long as you want. Sew the domes tog from the WS or join them as they are made by holding the RS of 2 domes tog and attaching them from the WS using a couple of sc sts. Using crochet hook and yarn A, sc around the edge of cuff to help bring colors tog and finish the project. Weave in ends.

Wristers

— Jennifer Claydon

These easy fingerless gloves, knit in fairly smooth handspun merino, display the qualities of handspun yarn beautifully. Only a small amount of yarn is needed, and the pattern looks lovely in both solid and variegated colors. Knit a pair to keep chilly winter breezes at bay, or gift some to a friend.

WRISTERS (MAKE 2)

Note: Knit piece from top down.

CO 28 sts. Place marker and join for working the round, being careful not to twist sts. Work in k2, p2 rib for 1" (3cm).

Knit 2 rnds. At end of second rnd, turn and purl back. Work flat in St st until piece measures 3" (8cm) from cast-on edge for thumb opening.

Resume working in the round in St st until piece measures 5½" (14cm) from cast-on edge.

Work in k2, p2 rib for 1" (3cm) more. Bind off.

Finishing

Weave in ends.

Materials

SIZES
Women's average

FINISHED MEASUREMENTS
7" (18cm) at cuff, unstretched

YARN
70 yds (64m) 2-ply handspun, approximately 9 wraps per inch

NEEDLES
Set of US size 8 (5.0mm) DPNs

NOTIONS
Tapestry needle
Stitch marker

GAUGE
16 sts and 26 rows = 4" (10cm) in St st

About Jennifer Claydon

Jennifer Claydon is a book editor by day, an author by night and a fiber artist at all times. Her love for spinning and fiber is reflected in her book, *Spin Dye Stitch*. Her current artistic endeavors include spinning gossamer-weight yarns that she knits into lace shawls of her own design. Jenni lives, loves and hoards fiber in Cincinnati. Her house made of wool also contains one very understanding husband and two rambunctious cats.

Fringed Scarf

— Jonelle Raffino and Prudence Mapstone

This scarf is designed for crochet-lovers. The body is knitted in textured seed stitch, while the fringe is a lovely array of crocheted ovals and circles that drape gracefully from chained fringe.

SCARF

With US 7 (4.5mm) needles, CO 41 sts.

Knit 1 row.

Knit 4 rows in seed st (k1, p1) across row to last st, k1.

Next row: K1, *yo, k2, sl yo over those 2 sts; rep from * across.

Next row: Purl.

Rep last 2 rows until scarf measures 49" (124cm) long.

Knit 4 rows in seed st as before. BO. Weave in ends.

FREEFORM EMBELLISHMENTS

Small Open Circles (make 6–10)

Wrap yarn A around your index finger a number of times to create a padded center. Slip the yarn off your finger, ch 1, and then work as many dc around the ring as it takes to fill it solidly enough so that it lies flat. Join with sl st. With yarn B, work a rnd of sl sts into the front loop of each of the dc, sl st to join and fasten off. Turn the piece over and work another rnd of sl sts into the back loops so B shows up on both sides of the scarf.

Large Open Circles (make 5–7)

Work as for Small Open Circles, adding an additional 1–2 rnds of dc before working contrast rounds, increasing as needed to keep motif flat.

Deluxe Reversible Oval Discs (make 25–30)

With crochet hook and yarn B, ch 3 and join with sl st to form a ring. Ch 1, and into the ring work 2 sc, 2 hdc, 4 dc, 2 hdc, 2 sc. Join with sl st, fasten off.

Join as follows: With yarn A, slip the crochet hook out of the loop, insert the hook into the back loop of the last dc worked on the other disc, pick up the loop again and pull it through. Ch 5, *dc into the back loops of the next st on both discs to join them together, ch 2. Rep from * around, sl st to join. Ch 1 and then work 3 or 4 hdc into each of the ch-2 spaces to create a solid rim around the motif. Sl st to join. Do not cut off yarn, but make a length of chain double the desired fringe length (between 60 to 100 ch). Skip the 1st ch and work 3 sc into the next ch.

Cont working 3 sc into each of the next 10 to 20 ch to create a corkscrew on the end of the fringe. When corkscrew is desired size, skip the next ch and sl st into the following ch. Fasten off and weave in ends.

With yarn B, work rnds of sl sts into the front loops of the dc sts around the motif. Then turn the motif over and do the same into the back loops that will now be facing you on the other side. Weave in ends.

Materials

SIZES
One size

FINISHED MEASUREMENTS
8" × 50" (20cm × 127cm)

YARN
6 skeins SWTC Inspiration (SOYSILK® /alpaca blend, 1.75oz/50g, 125yd/114m)

5 skeins in Color A

1 skein in Color B

NEEDLES AND HOOKS
US size 7 (4.5mm) straight knitting needles
Size F (3.75mm) crochet hook

NOTIONS
Tapestry needle

GAUGE
Knit: 20 sts = 4" (10cm) in patt
Crochet: 12 sts = 4" (10cm) in patt

Finishing

Arrange circles as desired at ends of scarf. Sew in place. To attach the fringe, fold each one off center so the disc and the corkscrew fall at different lengths, insert crochet hook into a st at the end of the scarf, pull through the ch at the fold point to create a loop, drop the ends of the fringe through the loop and pull down to secure. Attach remaining fringe in same manner, spaced evenly on both ends of the scarf.

Chapter
4

Socks and Stockings

What is it that makes sock knitting so addictive? Is it the practicality and comfort of soft, durable footwear? The variety of sock yarns, fibers and colors? Or maybe it's that socks are such small projects, they can be taken virtually anywhere.

An ideal place to take your sock projects is the local coffee shop. You can relax, converse with a friend and concentrate—just a little—on the lace or cable pattern. If you're in love with lace, try knitting the *Dancing Bamboo Socks* (page 106). If cables tickle your fancy, the *Traveling Stitch Socks* (page 100) might be perfect for you.

To keep your stitches from escaping, clamp a metal or plastic sock needle case over the double-pointed needles. Found in the notions section of most knitting shops, it's a handy little tool that's useful for all knitters on the go.

Ballerina Bliss Slippers

— Louise Butt and Kirstie McLeod

Get in touch with your inner diva and take a twirl in these gorgeous slippers. Modeled on the classic, elegant shape of ballet shoes, they're perfect for blissing out in your boudoir or just hanging out at home. Make the slippers in vibrant colors and experiment with embellishments—beads, buttons, sequins and embroidery. There are many ways to make your ballet shoes beautiful.

SLIPPERS (MAKE 2)

Sole

Cast on 12 (12, 14) sts using size 6 (4.0mm) needles.

Row 1: K.

Row 2: P1, pfb, k8 (8, 10), pfb, p1—14 (14, 16) sts.

Row 3: K.

Row 4: P1, pfb, k10 (10, 12), pfb, p1—16 (16, 18) sts.

Row 5: K.

Row 6: P1, pfb, k12 (12, 14), pfb, p1—18 (18, 20) sts.**
Work 53 (55, 57) rows in St st.

Next row: P1, p2tog, k12 (12, 14), p2tog tbl, p1—16 (16, 18) sts.

Next row: K.

Next row: P1, p2tog, k10 (10, 12), p2tog tbl, p1—14 (14, 16) sts.

Next row: K.

MORE➡

Materials

SIZES
S (M, L)

YARN
Approximately 175 yds (137m) DK acrylic yarn

NEEDLES AND HOOKS
US size 6 (4.0mm) straight knitting needles

Size G6 (4.0mm) crochet hook

NOTIONS
Artificial flower petals

Contrasting bead for center of flower

GAUGE
22 sts and 30 rows = 4" (10cm) in St st using size 6 (4.0mm) needles

Next row: P1, p2tog, k8 (8, 10), p2tog tbl, p1—12 (12, 14) sts.

Next row: K.

Bind off.

Top of Slipper

Work as for Sole to **.

Work 18 rows in St st.

Next row: K8 (8, 9) sts, bind off 2 sts, k8 (8, 9) sts—16 (16, 18) sts.

Next row: Working on first 8 (8, 9) sts only, p.

Next row: K2tog tbl, k to end—7 (7, 8) sts.

Next row: P.

Next row: K2tog tbl, k to end—6 (6, 7) sts.

Next row: P.

Work 10 (10, 12) rows in St st ending on P row.

Next row: K1, M1, k5 (5, 6) sts—7 (7, 8) sts.

Work 7 rows in St st.

Next row: K1, M1, k6 (6, 7) sts—8 (8, 9) sts.

Work 9 rows in St st.

Next row: K1, M1, k7 (7, 8) sts—9 (9, 10) sts.

Next row: P.

Bind off.

Rejoin yarn to rem sts and rep for other side, reversing shapings.

Assembly

With right sides facing, join Sole to Top of Slipper.

Crochet Edging

With size G6 (4.00mm) crochet hook, work a round of single crochet in a number divisible by 4.

Next round: Chain 1, work 2 sc into next 2 sts, *skip 1 st, work 3 sc, rep from * to end. Fasten off.

Add the petals of an artificial flower to the slipper and secure in place with a contrasting bead.

Strapping Style

Make some straps to help the slippers stay on your feet.

Knit the strap:

Cast on 3 sts.

Work in garter st (knit every row) until strap measures 5" (13cm).

Bind off.

Using the photograph as a guide, attach one side of the strap(s) to the inside of the slipper where the crochet edge meets the knitting edge.

Attach the other end to the outside of the slipper on the other side.

Finish by sewing a button onto the end of the strap.

Inspiration

Here is some inspiration for how you can embellish your slippers:

- *Using a contrasting yarn, embroider a spiral pattern.*

- *Add some matching buttons in a random pattern using a strong thread.*

- *Using strong sewing thread, attach beads in the shape of a snowflake.*

Adding straps also gives a different look, and the variations are endless. See page 94 for instructions on adding them.

Fishnet Stockings

— Dorothy Ratigan

Channel 1960s sophistication with a pair of sexy lace stockings. You'll have to do some fancy needlework to keep the correct stitch count, but the results are definitely worth it. Try knitting them in basic black for a classy night out, or punch them up with a bright pink or turquoise to wear to a concert. Pair with some high heels and a miniskirt, and you're ready to hit the town!

SPECIAL STITCHES

Fishnet Lace Pattern (multiple of 4 sts)

Rnd 1: *Yo, sl 2 tog kwise, k1, p2sso, yo, k1; rep from * to end of rnd.

Rnds 2 and 4: K all sts.

Rnd 3: Sl first st from Needle 1 to Needle 4. *Yo, k1, yo, sl 2 tog kwise, k1, p2sso; rep from * to end of rnd.

Note: When you get to the last 2 sts on each needle, you will have to move the first stitch from the next needle to this needle to complete the double decrease.

Rep Rnds 1–4 for patt.

K1, P1 Rib (multiple of 2 sts)

Rnd 1: *K1, p1; rep from * to end of rnd.

Rep Rnd 1 for patt.

MORE ➡

Materials

SIZES
Women's—customizable

FINISHED MEASUREMENTS
Approximately 8" (20cm) circumference, leg and foot length as desired

YARN
3 skeins Rowan 4 Ply Soft (100% merino wool, 1.75oz/50g, 191yd/175m) color #383

NEEDLES
Set of US size 5 (3.75mm) DPNs
Set of US size 3 (3.25mm) DPNs

NOTIONS
Tapestry needle

GAUGE
24 sts = 4" (10cm) in Fishnet Lace on larger needles, unstretched
28 sts = 4" (10cm) in St st on smaller needles

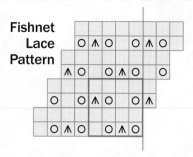

Fishnet Lace Pattern

knit

○ yarn over

⋀ slip 2 together knitwise, knit 1, pass 2 slipped stitches over the knit stitch

pattern repeat

SOCKS

Knit the Leg

Using the Long-Tail Cast On (see page 18) and larger DPNs, CO 48 sts and distribute evenly onto 4 DPNs. Join into a round, taking care not to twist the sts; change to smaller DPNs and work K1, P1 Rib for 1" (3cm).

Change to larger DPNs and beg Fishnet Lace Pattern. Continue until leg measures 13" (33cm) or desired length to top of heel.

Divide the Heel

With smaller DPNs, k 12 sts from Needle 1. Turn and p these 12 plus the 12 sts on Needle 4 onto the same needle. Work these sts back and forth with smaller DPNs. Leave rem 24 sts on hold for the instep.

Knit the Heel Flap

Row 1 (RS): *Sl 1 pwise, k1; rep from * to end, turn.

Row 2 (WS): Sl 1 pwise, p to end, turn.

Rep Rows 1–2 11 more times. You now have 12 chain sts along each side of the Heel Flap.

Turn the Heel

Row 1 (RS): K17, ssk, turn.

Row 2 (WS): Sl 1 pwise, p10, p2tog, turn.

Row 3: Sl 1 kwise, k10, ssk, turn.

Rep Rows 2–3 until all sts have been worked and 12 heel sts rem. End on a WS

row, sl the first and last sts of this row (see *This Sock's Secret* on page 99).

Knit the Gussets

With the same needle that holds the 12 heel sts, pick up and k 12 chain sts along one side of the Heel Flap.

With larger needle, work the instep sts in Fishnet Lace Pattern as est.

With smaller needle, pick up and k 12 chain sts along the other side of the Heel Flap and then k 6 heel sts onto the same needle.

You now have 18 sts on Needle 1 (smaller DPN), 12 sts each on Needles 2 and 3 (larger needles) and 18 sts on Needle 4 (smaller needle). Continue working gusset and sole sts in St st on smaller needles and instep sts in Fishnet Lace Pattern on larger needles.

Note: For Rnd 3 of Fishnet Lace Pattern, sl the first st onto the previous needle and pass the last st on that needle over this st. Work to last 2 sts, sl 1, k1, psso.

Shape the Gussets

Rnd 1: K to last 2 sts on Needle 1, k2tog; work instep sts in patt as est; ssk at beg of Needle 4, k to end of rnd.

Rnd 2: K gusset sts and work instep sts in est patt.

Rep Rnds 1–2 until 48 sts rem—12 sts on each needle.

Knit the Foot

Continue working sole in St st on smaller needles and instep in Fishnet Lace Pattern on larger needles until foot measures 7½" (19cm) from back of heel or 2" (5cm) less than desired finished measurement.

Shape the Toe

K all sts onto smaller DPNs, discontinuing Fishnet Lace Pattern and working all sts in St st.

Rnd 1: K to last 3 sts on Needle 1, k2tog, k1; k1, ssk at beg of Needle 2, k to end; k to last 3 sts on Needle 3, k2tog, k1; k1, ssk at beg of Needle 4, k to end.

Rnd 2: K all sts.

Rep Rnds 1–2 until 4 sts rem on each needle.

K 4 sts from Needle 1 onto Needle 4. Sl 4 sts from Needle 3 onto Needle 2.

Finishing

Kitchener stitch the two sets of 8 sts together.

Weave in ends. Wash and block the completed socks.

This Sock's Secret

A lace or openwork sock is lovely to knit and wear but won't hold up well to a lot of wear and tear unless you take special precautions. For added durability and comfort, knit the heel, toe and sole in a sturdier stitch, such as Stockinette stitch on a smaller needle.

About Dorothy Ratigan

Dorothy T. Ratigan's career in fiber arts spans thirty-five years, and in that time she's done it all. From bargello to beadwork, crewelwork, crochet, cross-stitch, embroidery, knitting, needlepoint, tatting and weaving, Dorothy has designed, stitched, edited and taught it all.

This adventure with needlework began with the skills that her mother, Peg, and her aunts, Nell and Delia, brought from Ireland and passed on to her. Dorothy has designed or edited for many major fiber magazines, craft book publishers and yarn companies. As president and co-owner of Pine Tree Knitters, she designed knitted skiwear, oversaw a production staff and marketed finished items to L.L.Bean, Eddie Bauer and others.

Dorothy has finally gotten to the bottom of her love of fiber with her recently published *Knitting the Perfect Pair: Secrets to Great Socks* (Krause Publications). Dorothy can be found at dorothyratigan@maine.rr.com.

Traveling Stitch Socks

— Dorothy Ratigan

Rustic and lovely, these traditional socks are perfect for wearing around the house on a rainy day. The cable and lace pattern looks difficult to complete, but it's easy to memorize and results in a pair of socks you'll be proud to show off.

Materials

SIZES
Women's—customizable

FINISHED MEASUREMENTS
Approximately 8" (20cm) circumference, leg and foot length as desired

YARN
2 skeins Cherry Tree Hill Yarn Supersock Solids (100% merino wool, 4oz/113g, 420yd/384m) color Natural

NEEDLES
Set of US size 1½ (2.5mm) DPNs, or three sizes smaller than larger needles
Set of US size 3 (3.25mm) DPNs
1 US size 3 (3.25mm) straight knitting needle

NOTIONS
Cable needle
Stitch marker
Tapestry needle

GAUGE
38 sts = 4" (10cm) in St st on larger needles

CABLING

C2L: Place next st on cn and hold in front of work, k1, k1b tbl from cn.

C2R: Place next st on cn and hold in back of work, k1 tbl, k st from cn.

PLC: Place next st on cn and hold in front, p1, k1 tbl from cn.

PRC: Place next st on cn and hold in back, k1 tbl, p1 from cn.

MORE ➡

Traveling Stitch Pattern

knit

–   purl

b   knit in back of stitch

╲   slip, slip, knit two stitches together through back loop

O   yarn over

╱   knit two stitches together

C2L place next stitch on cn and hold in front, k1, k1b from cn

C2R place next stitch on cn and hold in back, k1b, k1 from cn

PRC place next stitch on cn and hold in back, k1b, p1 from cn

PLC place next stitch on cn and hold in front, p1, k1b, from cn

Chart B

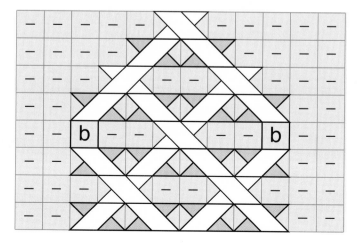

SPECIAL STITCHES

Twisted Rib

Rnd 1: *K1 tbl, p1; rep from * to end of rnd.

Rnd 2: *K1, p1 tbl; rep from * to end of rnd.

Rep Rnds 1–2 for patt.

Traveling Stitch Pattern

Chart A (worked over 25 sts)

Rnd 1: P1, k1 tbl, p2, ssk, yo, k1, p3, k2 tbl, p2, k2 tbl, p3, k1, yo, k2tog, p2, k1 tbl.

Rnds 2, 6 and 10: K1, k1 tbl, p2, k1, yo, k2tog, p3, C2L, p2, C2L, p3, ssk, yo, k1, p2, k1 tbl.

Rnds 3, 7 and 11: P1, k1 tbl, p2, ssk, yo, k1, p2, [PRC, PLC] twice, p2, k1, yo, k2tog, p2, k1 tbl.

Rnds 4 and 8: K1, k1 tbl, p2, k1, yo, k2tog, p2, k1 tbl, p2, C2L, p2, k1 tbl, p2, ssk, yo, k1, p2, k1 tbl.

Rnds 5 and 9: P1, k1 tbl, p2, ssk, yo, k1, p2, [PLC, PRC] twice, p2, k1, yo, k2tog, p2, k1 tbl.

Rnd 12: K1, k1 tbl, p2, k1, yo, k2tog, p2, k1 tbl, p2, C2L, p2, k1 tbl, p2, ssk, yo, k1, p2, k1 tbl.

Rnd 13: P1, k1 tbl, p2, ssk, yo, k1, p2, k1 tbl, p2, k2 tbl, p2, k1 tbl, p2, k1, yo, k2tog, p2, k1 tbl.

Rnd 14: K1, k1 tbl, p2, k1, yo, k2tog, p2, k1 tbl, p2, C2L, p2, k1 tbl, p2, ssk, yo, k1, p2, k1 tbl.

Rnds 15–20: Rep Rnds 13–14 3 times.

Chart B (worked over 12 sts)

Rnds 1 and 5: P2, [PLC, PRC] twice, p2.

Rnd 2: P3, C2L, p2, C2L, p3.

Rnd 3: P2, [PRC, PLC] twice, p2.

Rnd 4: P2, k1 tbl, p2, C2L, p2, k1 tbl, p2.

Rnd 6: P3, C2L, p2, C2R, p3.

Rnd 7: P4, PLC, PRC, p4.

Rnd 8: P5, C2L, p5.

SOCKS

Knit the Cuff

Using the Patterned Cast On (see page 19) and a straight needle, CO 76 sts in K1, P1 rib. Distribute sts evenly onto 4 smaller needles and join into a round, taking care not to twist the sts. Pm for beg of rnd.

Note: Round begins at center back.

Work Twisted Rib for 1¾" (4cm). Dec 1 st on the last rnd—75 sts.

Knit the Leg

Change to larger DPNs and divide sts evenly onto 3 needles. Work Rnds 1–20 of Traveling Stitch Pattern, Chart A. Rep Rnds 5–20 (16-rnd rep) 3 more times and then work Rnds 5–12 once or until leg measures 8½" (22cm) below the ribbing or desired length to top of the heel. Cut yarn.

Divide for the Heel

Sl 19 sts from Needle 1 to Needle 3. Join yarn.

Set-up row (WS): P37, place all rem sts onto Needle 2, turn. Work the heel flap back and forth on these 37 sts. Leave rem 38 sts on hold for the instep.

Knit the Heel Flap

Row 1 (RS): *Sl 1 pwise, k1 tbl; rep from * to last st, bring yarn to front of work, sl last st pwise.

Row 2 (WS): P all sts.

Rep Rows 1–2 14 more times. You now have 15 chain sts on each edge of the heel flap.

Turn the Heel

Row 1 (RS): K22, ssk, k1, turn.

Row 2 (WS): Sl 1 pwise, p8, p2tog, p1, turn.

Row 3: Sl 1 kwise, k9, ssk, k1, turn.

Row 4: Sl 1 pwise, p10, p2tog, p1, turn.

Continue in this manner, working 1 more st before the dec on every row until all heel sts have been worked and 23 sts rem. K 1 RS row, sl the first and last sts of this row.

Knit the Gussets

Note: Pick up and k through both loops of chain sts.

With the same needle that holds the heel sts, pick up and k 15 chain sts along one side of the Heel Flap and 1 st in the corner before instep sts.

With a new needle, work the 38 instep sts in Traveling Stitch Pattern as est; with a new needle, pick up and k 1 st in the corner after instep sts and 15 chain sts along other side of the Heel Flap and then k 11 heel sts onto same needle—93 sts.

Shape the Gussets

Rnd 1: K to last 2 sts on Needle 1, k2tog, p1 from Needle 2 onto Needle 1; work instep sts in patt as est on Needle 2 to last st, p last st onto Needle 3; ssk at the beg of Needle 3, k to end.

Rnd 2: K Gusset sts and work instep sts in patt as est, maintaining 1 p st on each side of instep sts.

Rnd 3: K to last 3 sts on Needle 1, k2tog, p1; work instep sts in patt on Needle 2; p1, ssk at beg of Needle 3, k to end.

Rep Rnds 2–3 until 75 sts rem, 19 sts on Needle 1, 38 sts on Needle 2, and 18 sts on Needle 3. Work 1 rnd even, inc 1 st on Needle 3—76 sts.

Knit the Foot

Continue working sole sts in St st, maintaining 1 p st on each side of instep sts, and instep sts in Traveling Stitch Pattern until foot measures 7½" (19cm) from back of Heel, or 2" (5cm) less than desired finished measurement, ending on patt Rnd 20.

Shape the Toe

Rnd 1 (dec rnd): K to last 3 sts on Needle 1, ssk, p1; at beg of Needle 2, p1, k2tog, k10, work Chart B over next 12 sts, k to last 3 sts on Needle 2, ssk, p1; p1, k2tog at beg of Needle 3, k to end.

Rnd 2: Work even in est patt.

Rnd 3 (dec rnd): K to last 3 sts on Needle 1, ssk, p1; at beg of Needle 2, p1, k2tog, k9, work Chart B over next 12 sts, k to last 3 sts on Needle 2, ssk, p1; p1, k2tog at beg of Needle 3, k to end.

Rnd 4: Work even in est patt.

Continue in this manner, working one fewer st before and after Chart B sts on each dec rnd six more times—44 sts. Work dec rnd only five times—24 sts. With Needle 3, k across 6 sts on Needle 1.

Finishing

Kitchener stitch the two sets of 12 sts together. Weave in ends. Wash and block the completed socks.

Avoiding Rabbit Ears

When working a common heel like the one used in this pattern, there are sometimes stitches that stick out on both ends of the heel. These stitches are called rabbit ears. To prevent these, slip the first and last stitches of the last heel row.

Dancing Bamboo Socks

— *Holly Daymude*

There's no doubt about it: these socks have an inherent "wow" factor. Knit in a soft merino/tencel blend in an eye-catching color, you'll blaze through the easy lace pattern and simple construction. Perhaps the biggest "wow" of all is how quickly you'll knit them up!

Materials

SIZES
Women's—customizable

FINISHED MEASUREMENTS
8" (20cm) foot circumference

YARN
1 skein C*Eye*Ber Fiber Merino Tencel Fingering Weight (superwash merino/Tencel blend, 4oz/114g, 410yd/375m) color Crimson and Clover

NEEDLES
2 24" (61cm) US size 1 (2.25mm) circular knitting needles

NOTIONS
Tapestry needle
Stitch markers

GAUGE
32 sts and 40 rows = 4" (10cm) in St st

SOCKS

Leg

CO 64 sts. Divide sts evenly over both needles. Pm and join, being careful not to twist.

Work in k2, p2 ribbing for 1" (3cm).

Setup rnd: *P1, k6, p1; rep from * around.

Bamboo Pattern

Work bamboo patt as foll below or using the chart on page 108.

Rnd 1: *P1, yo, ssk, k4, p1; rep from * around.

Rnd 2 (and all even rnds to 10): *P1, k6, p1; rep from * around.

Rnd 3: *P1, k1, yo, ssk, k3, p1; rep from * around.

Rnd 5: *P1, k2, yo, ssk, k2, p1; rep from * around.

Rnd 7: *P1, k3, yo, ssk, k1, p1; rep from * around.

Rnd 9: *P1, k4, yo, ssk, p1; rep from * around.

MORE➔

Bamboo Chart

Key

\	ssk
(blank box)	knit
–	purl
0	yarn over

–	\	0						–		9
–		\	0					–		7
–			\	0				–		5
–				\	0			–		3
–					\	0		–		1

Note: Even-numbered rows are not charted. Work even-numbered rows in pattern as established.

Rep Rnds 1–10 until leg measures 10" (25cm) or desired length, ending with Rnd 10.

Heel Flap

Working on 32 sts for heel, leaving instep sts on hold, cont as foll:

Row 1 (RS): *Sl 1, k1; rep from * to end of row.

Row 2: *Sl 1, purl; rep from * to end of row.

Rep Rows 1–2 a total of 14 times.

Turn Heel

Row 1: K18, ssk, k1, turn.

Row 2: Sl 1, p5, p2tog, p1, turn.

Row 3: Sl 1, k6, ssk, k1, turn.

Row 4: Sl 1, p7, p2tog, p1, turn.

Cont shaping the heel in this manner, working 1 more st before each dec, ending with:

Row 13: K16, ssk, k1, turn.

Row 14: P17, p2tog, p1, turn—19 sts.

Gusset

Knit across the 19 Heel sts.

Using the same needle, pick up 14 sts along the Heel Flap (1 st in each slipped st along the flap), make 1 additional st in the space between the Gusset and the instep sts.

Using the 2nd needle, work in patt across the instep sts.

Using the 1st needle again, make 1 st in the space between the instep and Gusset, pick up 14 sts along the Heel Flap.

K9 heel sts, pm to mark new start of rnd.

Rnd 1: K9 sts, knit rem Heel sts tbl to the last 2 sts, k2tog. Work in patt across the instep. Ssk, knit rem Heel sts tbl to the last 9 sts, k9.

Rnd 2: Knit.

Rep Rnds 1–2 until there are 65 sts.

Foot

Cont in patt across the instep and in St st across the sole with no additional dec until sock measures approx 2" (5cm) less than desired length.

Setup rnd: Knit.

Toe

Rnd 1: *K1, ssk, knit to last 3 sts on the 1st needle, k2tog, k1; rep from * once more on second needle.

Rnd 2: Knit.

Rep Rnds 1–2 until there are 25 sts.

Graft the sts tog using Kitchener st.

Rep to make a second sock.

Finishing

Weave in ends.

About Holly Daymude

Holly Daymude is the retail manager of Knit Happens, an LYS in Alexandria, Virginia. She has been knitting for about five years. She loves knitting socks and always has a few pairs on the needles. Holly's favorite pasttime, other than knitting, is knitting and drinking wine.

Chapter 5

Other Favorites

Take-along knitting isn't limited to winter accessories, and this chapter proves it. A trio of *Fruity Bibs* (page 112), a *Sock Knitting Needle Roll* (page 118) and even a pair of knitted *Leaf Earrings* (page 126) are just some of the portable projects you'll find.

When choosing a project to take with you, don't be limited by thinking that the size of a finished project is a factor. Sweaters constructed in several pieces can be knitted one section at a time and then seamed and blocked at home. The same can be said of blankets or afghans that are knitted square by square and then sewn together later. You'll be amazed at the amount of knitting you can complete when you take it along—use your imagination, and the possibilities are endless!

Fruity Bibs

— Heidi Boyd

These darling bibs are colorful, practical and easy to make. The intarsia technique adds a fun motif to the center of each bib—it's a great chance to learn this colorwork staple if you haven't already. A trio of bibs, with a different motif on each one, makes a great gift for an expecting mom.

Materials

SIZES

One size

FINISHED MEASUREMENTS

Strawberry and cherry: approximately 8¾" × 7¾" (21cm × 20cm)

Daisy: approximately 7½" × 4½" (19cm × 11cm)

YARN

1 skein each Classic Elite Bam Boo (100% bamboo, 1.75oz/50g, 77yd/70m) color #4915 Bamboo Leaf (A), color #4919 Flamingo (B) and color #4988 Melon (C)

Note: One skein of each color makes the three-bib set.

NEEDLES

US size 7 (4.5mm) straight knitting needles

NOTIONS

Stitch markers

Stitch holder

3 ⅝" (16mm) buttons

Tapestry needle

GAUGE

18 sts and 31 rows = 4" (10cm) in garter st

BIBS

Note: When working from charts, be sure to twist yarns together at color changes to prevent gaps. (See page 35 for step-by-step instructions on intarsia.)

Cherry Bib

With yarn C, CO 40 sts. Knit 1 row.

Change to yarn B. Cont in garter st for 18 rows.

Next row (RS): K15, pm, work Row 1 of Cherry Chart over next 10 sts in St st, pm, k15.

Next row (WS): K15, sm, work Row 2 of Cherry Chart over next 10 sts in St st, sm, k15.

Cont as set for 14 rows of Cherry Chart.

After completing chart, remove markers.

Cont in garter st for 14 rows.

MORE➤

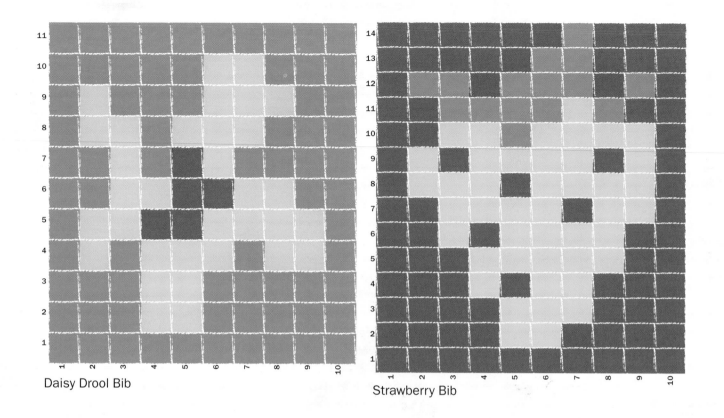

Daisy Drool Bib

Strawberry Bib

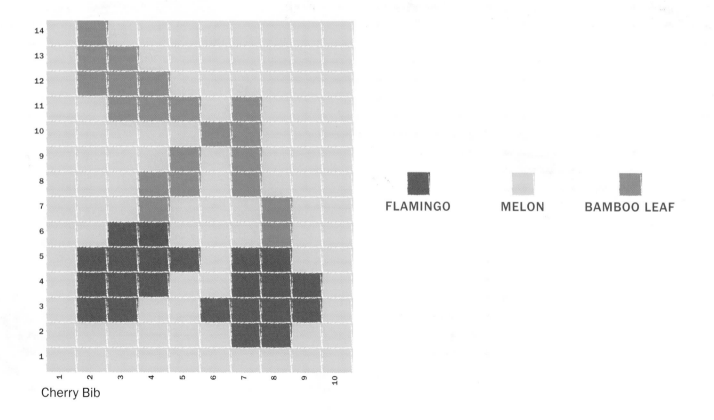

Cherry Bib

FLAMINGO   MELON   BAMBOO LEAF

114

Change to A. Knit 1 row.

Next row (WS): K15 and place these sts on holder, BO 10, k15.

Neck Tab

Next row: Knit to last 2 sts, k2tog.

Next row: Knit.

Rep last 2 rows 4 times more—10 sts.

BO all sts.

Neck Strap

Transfer 15 held sts to needle and rejoin yarn at neck edge.

Next row: Knit.

Next row: Knit to last 2 sts, k2tog.

Rep last 2 rows 4 times more—10 sts.

Cont in garter st for 9" (23cm).

Buttonhole Row: K4, yo, k2tog, k4.

Knit 1 row.

K2tog at beg of next 2 rows—8 sts.

BO all sts.

Strawberry Bib

With yarn A, CO 40 sts. Knit 1 row.

Change to yarn C. Cont in garter st for 18 rows.

Next row (RS): K15, pm, work Row 1 of Strawberry Chart over next 10 sts in St st, pm, k15.

Next row (WS): K15, sm, work Row 2 of Strawberry Chart over next 10 sts in St st, sm, k15.

Cont as set for 14 rows of Strawberry Chart, keeping center 10 sts in St st.

After completing chart, remove markers.

Cont in garter st for 14 rows.

Change to yarn B. Knit 1 row.

Next row (WS): K15 and place these sts on holder, BO 10, k15.

Work Neck Tab and Neck Strap as for Cherry Bib.

Daisy Drool Bib

With yarn B, CO 34 sts. Knit 1 row.

Change to yarn A. Cont in garter st for 6 rows.

MORE➜

Yarn Selection

If you're looking for a sturdier bib for older babies, you might consider substituting a stiffer yarn.

115

Next row (RS): K12, pm, work Row 1 of Daisy Chart over next 10 sts in St st, pm, k12.

Next row (WS): K12, sm, work Row 2 of Daisy Chart over next 10 sts in St st, sm, k12.

Cont as set for 11 rows of Daisy Chart, keeping center 10 sts in St st.

After completing chart, remove markers.

Cont in garter st for 10 rows.

Change to yarn C. Knit 1 row.

Next row (WS): K12 and place these sts on holder, BO 10, k12.

Neck Tab

Next row: Knit to last 2 sts, k2tog.

Knit 1 row.

Rep last 2 rows 3 times more—8 sts.

BO all sts.

Neck Strap

Transfer 12 held sts to needle and rejoin yarn at neck edge.

Next row: Knit.

Next row: Knit to last 2 sts, k2tog.

Rep last 2 rows 3 times more—8 sts.

Cont in garter st for 6" (15cm).

Buttonhole row: K3, yo, k2tog, k3.

Knit 1 row.

K2tog at beg of next 2 rows—6 sts.

BO all sts.

Finishing (All)

Weave in ends. Stitch a button to the Neck Tab, aligning it with the buttonhole.

Sock Knitting Needle Roll

— *Jane Davis*

Here's a project that will certainly serve you for years to come. The *Sock Knitting Needle Roll* is basically a knitted rectangle that is fulled and shaped and then lined in a contrasting fabric. If you regularly take your knitting on the go, this case will prove a worthy friend: Tuck it into your purse before you leave, and you'll always have the correct needle size at your fingertips!

CASE

CO 60 sts. Work in St st until piece measures 13" (33cm). BO. Weave in ends.

Fulling

Steam block the knitted rectangle so it lies flat. Full the knitted fabric (see *Fulling Knitted and Crocheted Fabric*, page 38). When the piece is fulled, rinse out the soapy water and lay the piece flat to dry. When the piece is dry, fold it in thirds and steam press to set the folds.

MORE➡

Materials

SIZES
One size

FINISHED MEASUREMENTS
Before fulling: Approximately 13" (33cm) wide by 10½" (27cm) tall

After fulling: Approximately 9" (23cm) wide by 8" (20cm) tall

YARN
1 skein Araucania Atacama (100% alpaca, 1.75oz/50g, 110 yd/100m) color #522

NEEDLES
US size 4 (3.5mm) straight knitting needles

NOTIONS
12" (30cm) piece of 44" (112cm) fabric for lining, or 1 fat quarter

Tapestry needle

12" (30cm) single-fold bias tape

¾" (2cm) button

Straight pins

Steam iron

Sewing machine

Sewing thread to match fabric

FULLING SUPPLIES
Bubble wrap

Hot, soapy water

Dowel rod

Rubber bands

GAUGE
23 sts and 29 rows = 4" (10cm) in St st, before fulling

Lining

Cut a piece of fabric for the lining to measure ½" (1cm) larger than the fulled rectangle on all sides.

Cut a second piece of fabric for the pocket to measure 12" (30cm) long and the same width as the lining. Fold the pocket in half lengthwise and press. Fold the bias tape over the folded edge of the pocket and topstitch.

Lay the pocket RS up on the RS of the lining, matching raw edges, and pin in place. Make channels for sock needles by sewing through all layers, spacing the lines of stitching ½"

(1cm) apart, or more for larger size needles.

Turn under all raw edges ½" (1cm) and press. Lay the lining on top of the fulled rectangle and stitch in place around the edges and along the fold lines in the fulled fabric.

Sew a button on one of the short edges. Make a button loop with thread opposite the button.

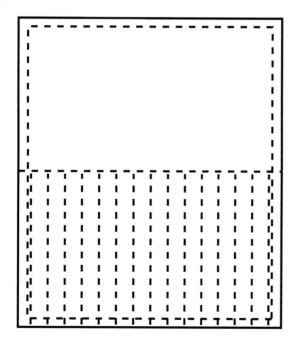

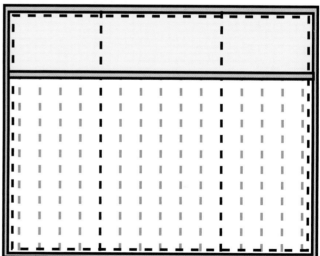

Baby Diamond

— *Helen Stewart*

Knits for babies are great portable projects because they're usually simple and, of course, small. This sweater, knit in a snuggly extrafine merino, can be knit for either a boy or a girl. The lace pattern along the edge provides just enough interest to the piece, and the top-down construction makes it easy to fit to any baby.

Materials

SIZES

0–3 (3–6, 9–12) months

FINISHED MEASUREMENTS

Chest: 16 (20½, 22¾)" [41 (52, 58)cm]

Length from shoulder: 10½ (12, 13½)" [27 (30, 34)cm]

YARN

2 (2, 2) skeins Grignasco Bambi (100% extrafine merino wool, 1.75oz/50g, 245yd/224m) color #185, light green

NEEDLES

16" (40cm) US size 4 (3.5mm) circular knitting needle

16" (40cm) US size 3 (3.25mm) circular knitting needle

Set of US size 4 (3.5mm) DPNs

Set of US size 3 (3.25mm) DPNs

NOTIONS

4 removable stitch markers

1 regular stitch marker

1 button

GAUGE

28 sts and 38 rows = 4" (10cm) in St st with larger needles

SWEATER

Yoke

Note: The yoke is knit back and forth to create the neck placket opening, and then the remainder of the sweater is worked in the round.

With smaller circular needle, CO 76 (88, 92) sts. Do not join.

Rows 1–6: Knit.

Change to larger circular needle.

Row 7 (RS): Pm for raglan shaping as follows: K12 (14, 15) for left front, yo, k1, place removable marker in the st just knit, yo, k12 (14, 14) for left sleeve, yo, k1, pm in st just knit, yo, k24 (28, 30) for back, yo, k1, pm in st just knit, yo, k12 (14, 14) for right sleeve, yo, k1, pm in st just knit, yo, k12 (14, 15) for right front—84 (96, 100) sts.

Note: You should have 4 marked sts with yarn overs on either side.

MORE➤

Diamond Lace Chart

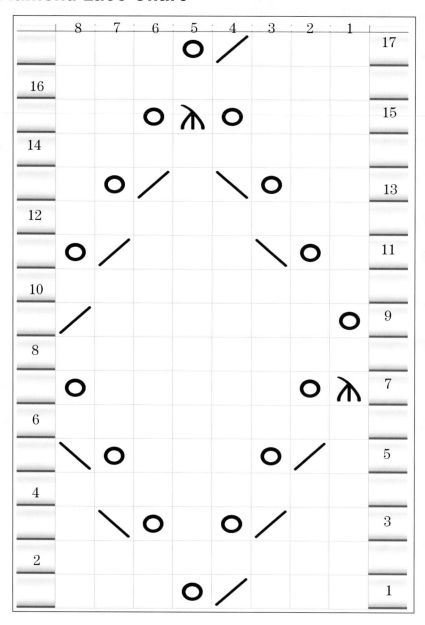

Legend

☐	Knit	\	ssk
/	k2tog	⋏	sl1 k2tog psso
O	yo		

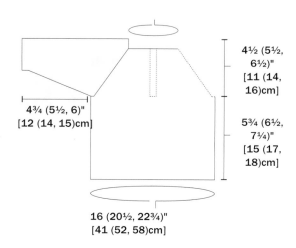

10¾ (12½, 13¼)"
[27 (32, 34)cm]

4½ (5½, 6½)"
[11 (14, 16)cm]

4¾ (5½, 6)"
[12 (14, 15)cm]

5¾ (6½, 7¼)"
[15 (17, 18)cm]

16 (20½, 22¾)"
[41 (52, 58)cm]

Row 8: K3, purl to last 3 sts, k3.

Row 9: *Knit to first marker, yo, k1, move removable marker in st just knit, yo; rep from * 3 times more, knit to end—8 sts inc.

Rep Rows 8–9 13 (18, 21) times more and then Row 8 only once—196 (248, 276) sts.

Separate Body and Sleeves

Next row (RS): Removing markers as you come to them, k28 (35, 39) sts, place next 42 (54, 60) sts on holder, use backward-loop method to CO 0 (2, 2) sts for underarm, k56 (70, 78) sts, place next 42 (54, 60) sts on holder, CO 0 (2, 2) sts for underarm, k28 (35, 39) sts—112 (144, 160) sts rem on needle.

Join for working in the rnd. K28 (36, 40) sts, pm at underarm. This is the beg of the rnd from now on.

Body

Work in St st until body measures 2¾ (3½, 4¼)" [7 (9, 11)cm] from underarm.

Work Rnds 1–17 of Diamond Lace Chart. Note that on Rnd 7 only, you will need to shift the beg of the rnd back by 1 st to accommodate the first sl 1-k2tog-psso.

After chart is complete, work 4 rnds even in St st.

Change to smaller circular needle and work 8 rnds in garter st (knit and purl alternate rnds). BO loosely.

Sleeves (make 2)

Place 42 (54, 60) held sts on larger DPNs. Pick up and k 1 st from underarm, pm for beg of rnd, pick up and k 1 st—44 (56, 62) sts.

Work 6 rnds even in St st.

Next rnd: K1, k2tog, knit to last 3 sts, ssk, k1—2 sts dec.

Rep last 7 rnds 4 (5, 6) times more—34 (44, 48) sts.

Work 6 (6, 3) rnds even.

Change to smaller DPNs and work in garter st for 6 rnds. BO loosely.

Finishing

Weave in ends. Block. Make button loop at top of neck opening and sew on button opposite.

About Helen Stewart

Helen, originally from Brisbane Australia, has lived in France, Singapore, Germany and now lives in London with her husband and baby daughter. A life-long crafter, Helen turned her hand to knitting in the early 2000s and finds knitting for babies and children particularly satisfying.

Helen met the Knitchicks in 2004 and instantly clicked with their sense of style and desire to simplify patterns though knitting in the round and eliminating unnecessary seams! Her first pattern appeared in *The Knitchicks' Guide to Sweaters*, which was published in 2009.

Leaf Earrings

~~~~~~

— Samantha Lopez

Who says all knitting needs to be with yarn? These earrings are a wonderful way to introduce yourself to the technique of knitting with wire. It's more challenging because of the tiny needles and unfamiliar materials, but the results are both striking and lovely. Be prepared to brag a little: You'll definitely be asked where you got your earrings when you wear them out!

Materials

SIZES

One size

WIRE

30-gauge Argentium or sterling silver wire (about 6' [183cm]) cut into 2 3' (91cm) pieces

30-gauge gold wire—1 each for the wrapping and sewing (about 10' [305cm]) cut into 2 5' (152cm) pieces

2 French ear wires 0.028" (.7mm) approximately 1" × ½" (2.5cm × 1cm)

NEEDLES

US size 0000 (1.25mm) straight knitting needles

NOTIONS

Needle- or round-nose pliers

Wire cutters

Clear epoxy or jewelers' cement

Toothpick or pin (for placement of epoxy)

Jewelers' tweezers

~~~~~~~~~~~~~~~~~~~~~~~~~~~~~~~~~~

EARRINGS (MAKE 2)

Cast on 1 st.

Row 1: K1.

Row 2: P1.

Row 3: Kfb = 2.

Row 4: P2.

Row 5: Kfb twice = 4.

Row 6: P4.

Row 7: Kfb, k2, kfb = 6.

Row 8: P6.

Row 9: Kfb, k4, kfb = 8.

Row 10: P8.

MORE➔

Row 11: Kfb, k6, kfb = 10.

Row 12: P10.

Row 13: K10.

Row 14: P10.

Row 15: K2tog, k6, k2tog = 8.

Row 16: P2tog, p4, p2tog = 6.

Row 17: K2tog, k2, k2tog = 4.

Row 18: P2tog, p2tog = 2.

Row 19: K2tog.

Row 20: P1.

Add ear wires while binding off (if soldered closed).

Complete the Earrings

Wrap each of the earrings with gold wire. Start at the point where the silver wire was bound off—the last loop containing the ear wire. Add the new gold wire by straddling the inside and outside edges of the loop and the trailing silver wire and then wrapping over, making sure to include the new end of gold wire. Continue to wrap until all edges are covered, including the ear-wire loop. (Note: If using ear wires that have been soldered closed, it will be necessary to wrap through the ear wire in order to continue wrapping around it.) Clip the gold wire close to the piece, tuck in with tweezers and apply a drop of epoxy.

Main Vein

Once the first piece is wrapped, cut a length of gold wire to about 18" (46cm). Temporarily wrap one end of the wire around the top loop containing the ear wire. Run the loose end along the middle of the leaf to the other end lengthwise. Sew the wire around the wrapped edge of this bottom loop and then pass it under and over the new gold "vein," starting the wrapping. As you wrap, occasionally pick up one of the silver wire loops underneath so the vein is stitched to the leaf. Continue until the last 3 stitches that make up the "stem" are reached. Unwrap the end from the edge of the loop at the top and sew around the bottom of the third stitch from the top. Cut and tuck. With the loose end, wrap to the end, cut, tuck and place a small bead of epoxy to seal.

Side Veins

Cut a piece of wire about 6" (15cm) long. Beginning on the knit side of the leaf, sew the wire under the middle vein about 3 stitches down from the bottom of the "stem" and pull it back through to the front on the other side so that half of this new wire is now on either side of the middle vein. Secure one end by loosely wrapping it over the edge. Run the loose end diagonally across the knitting to the edge, making sure it lies relatively parallel to the bottom of the leaf on that same side. Sew wire around the edge, passing under and around the new diagonal vein for the first wrap. Continue in this manner, picking up some of the "leaf" stitches along the way, until you reach the middle vein. Cut, tuck and glue. Repeat with the opposite loose end, ending with an elongated V.

Repeat this process to create two more veins, this time beginning 5 stitches from the center of the V along the main vein, making sure the new veins parallel the others.

Repeat the entire veining process for the second earring.

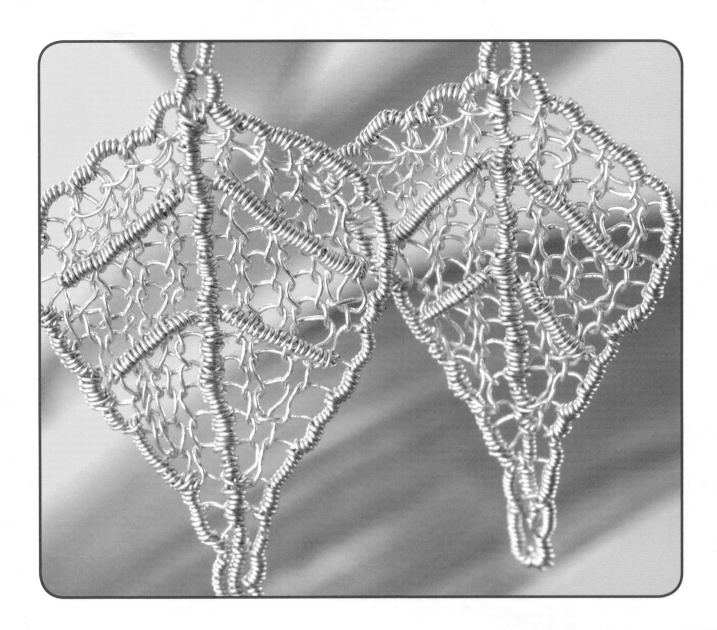

About Samantha Lopez

Samantha's work has been exhibited at the Rubelle and Norman Schafler Gallery and Object Image Gallery in Brooklyn, New York. Pieces have also been featured in online publications and the Swedish magazine *XOXO* as well as the Mun2 TV show *Vivo*. Most recently, a book on her interpretation of jewelry, *Knitted Wire Jewelry*, was published by North Light Books. She currently lives in Brooklyn, New York with her husband/creative consultant, Richard, and their rescued pit bull, Amazing.

Her line of jewelry can be found online at www.knotstudio.com as well as in select boutiques and galleries in the New York City area.

Reversible Striped Bag

— Jane Davis

As most knitters know, the brand Noro evokes images of rich, luxurious color and dazzling striping effects. This striped and fulled handbag takes full advantage of the qualities Noro has become famous for, resulting in a gorgeous and sturdy tote that's great for carrying needles and yarn.

Materials

SIZES

One size

FINISHED MEASUREMENTS

Before fulling: approximately 14½" (37cm) wide and 14" (36cm) tall when flat, not including handles

After fulling: approximately 11½" (29cm) wide and 11" (28cm) tall when flat, not including handles

YARN

4 skeins Noro Kureyon (100% wool, 1.75oz/50g, 110yd/101m)

   2 skeins in color A
   1 skein each in colors B and C

NEEDLES

29" (74cm) US size 10½ (6.5mm) circular knitting needle

2 US size 10½ (6.5mm) DPNs

NOTIONS

Stitch marker

Tapestry needle

Pearl cotton

FULLING SUPPLIES

Washing machine

Dishwashing soap

GAUGE

16 sts and 20 rows = 4" (10cm) in St st, before fulling

BAG

With Color A and circular needle, CO 100 sts. Pm and join for working in the round. K 74 rnds, alternating 2 rnds A and 2 rnds B, replacing B with C when B is used up.

Bag Base

Continuing with A only, dec as follows:

Rnd 1: *K2, k2tog; rep from * to end—75 sts.

Rnd 2: Knit all sts.

Rnd 3: *K1, k2tog; rep from * to end—50 sts.

Rnd 4: Knit all sts.

Rnd 5: *K2tog; rep from * to end—25 sts.

MORE➡

Rnd 6: Knit all sts.

Cut yarn, leaving a 12" (30cm) tail. Thread tapestry needle with tail and pass through all rem sts, pulling them off the knitting needle as you pick them up with the tapestry needle. Pull the sts tight to close the opening. Pass the tail through the sts once more and fasten off. Weave in ends.

I-Cord Straps (Make 2)

Using 2 DPNs and yarn color of your choice, CO 7 sts, leaving a 12" (30cm) tail. K across the row. *Do not turn work, but keeping the RS facing you, slide the sts back to the right end of needle. Pull the working yarn across the back of the knitting and k across the row again. Repeat from * until knitting measures 12" (30cm). BO and cut yarn, leaving a 12" (30cm) tail.

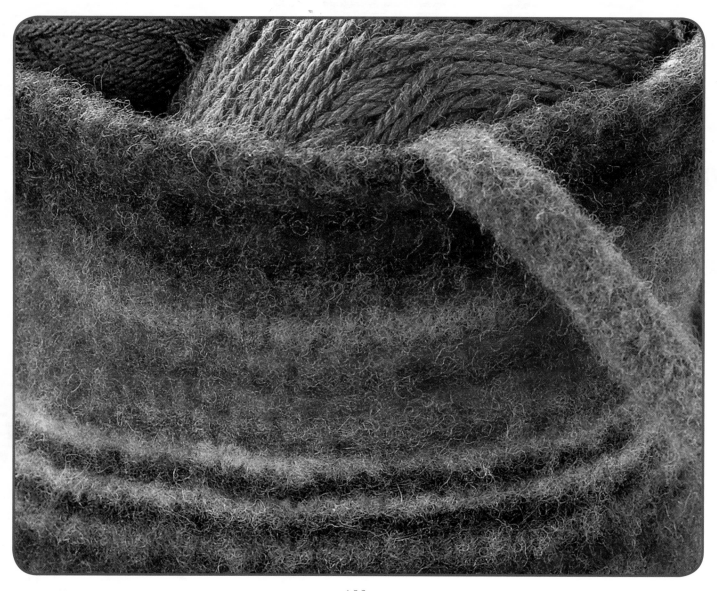

Knit side of fulled fabric

Purl side of fulled fabric

Assembly

Using a tapestry needle and a 36" (91cm) length of yarn, roll the top edge of the bag to the RS and whipstitch in place, approximately 6 rows down from the edge.

Using the yarn tails on the straps, sew the straps to the top of the bag, placing the ends of the straps about 4" (10cm) apart.

Fulling

Using the pearl cotton, baste the top of the bag closed. Throw the bag in the washer on the hot/cold setting and the lowest water level with some dishwashing soap (see *Fulling Knitted and Crocheted Fabric*, page 38). Check every 5–10 minutes to see if the fulling process is complete. When the bag is completely fulled, remove the basting, shape the bag and let it dry.

Openwork Handbag

— Stefanie Japel

As any fashionista knows, looking glamorous is all in the accessories. Play up your inner bombshell with this elegant evening bag, knit in a neutral golden tan that will complement your evening attire. The lace pattern is interesting and easy to learn, making this project perfect for knitting on the go.

PURSE

Lace Pattern

Work lace patt over a multiple of 10 sts + 7.

Rows 1, 3, 5 and 7 (RS): K2, [p1, k1] twice, *k2tog, yo, k1, yo, ssk, [k1, p1] twice, k1; rep from * to last st, k1.

Rows 2, 4, 6 and 8: P3, *k1, p9; rep from * to last 4 sts, k1, p3.

Rows 9, 11, 13 and 15: K1, k2tog, yo, k1, yo, ssk, *[k1, p1] twice, k1, k2tog, yo, k1, yo, ssk; rep from * to last st, k1.

Rows 10, 12, 14 and 16: P8, *k1, p9; rep from * to last 9 sts, k1, p8.

Rep Rows 1–16.

Body

Cast on 47 sts. Work in St st for 1" (3cm), ending with a RS row. Knit 1 row (turning row). Work 48 rows in lace patt (3 vertical patt rep). Purl 1 row (turning row). Work in St st for 1" (3cm). Bind off.

Finishing

Fold the knitted piece in half longways with WS together. Seam the sides.

Fold the lining fabric in half longways with WS together. With a sewing machine, seam the sides using a ½" (1cm) seam allowance.

Fold the top 1" (3cm) of the lining to the inside and press it flat. Place the lining inside the knit piece. Fold the knit piece to the inside at the turning row, with the top of the lining under the fold, and seam it, making sure the sts catch the outside knit fabric of the purse.

Attach the handles to the top of the purse body with leather cord, making sure the cord catches inside and outside the fabric of the purse, as well as the lining.

Materials

SIZES

One size

FINISHED MEASUREMENTS

7" × 16" (18cm × 41cm), excluding purse frame

YARN

1 hank Kollage Illumination (mohair/viscose/polyamide blend, 2.75oz/78g, 150yd/137m), color Hazelnut

NEEDLES

US size 11 (8.0mm) straight knitting needles

NOTIONS

1 piece 17" × 16" (43cm × 41cm) fabric for lining

1 pair plastic purse handles from Sunbelt Fastener

1 yd (1m) leather cord

Sewing machine

Sewing needle and thread

GAUGE

11 sts and 13½ rows = 4" (10cm) in lace patt

Resources and Information

Though we couldn't possibly fit every piece of knitting information within these last few pages, we've done our best to provide a comprehensive knitting resource section to help you complete your take-along projects. From a glossary that defines common knitting abbreviations to a list of the yarn companies featured in this book, this section will untangle your toughest knitting questions.

Resources

Araucania
www.araucaniayarns.com
Sock Knitting Needle Roll, *Felting the Complete Guide*

Cascade Yarns
http://cascadeyarns.com
Stretchy I-Cord Hats, *Soft and Simple Knits for Little Ones*
Silky Smoke Ring, *Knit One, Embellish Too*

C*Eye*Ber Fiber
www.ceyeberfiberyarns.com
Dancing Bamboo Socks, *Pints and Purls*

Cherry Tree Hill Yarn
802.525.3311
http://cherryyarn.com
Traveling Stitch Socks, *Knitting the Perfect Pair*

Classic Elite Yarns
http://classiceliteyarns.com
Fruity Bibs, *Soft and Simple Knits for Little Ones*

Harrisville Designs
www.harrisville.com
Fedora Hat, *Felting The Complete Guide*

JaggerSpun
www.jaggeryarn.com
Lacy Accent Scarf, *Glam Knits*

Karabella Yarns
800.550.0898
http://karabellayarns.com
Sideways Scarf, *Pints and Purls*
Cashmere Ruffles Scarf, *Closely Knit*

Kollage
http://kollageyarns.com
Openwork Handbag, *Glam Knits*

Louisa Harding
www.knittingfever.com
Sparkling Leaves Spring Hat, *Beautiful Embroidered and Embellished Knits*

Noro
http://noroyarns.com
Reversible Striped Bag, *Felting The Complete Guide*

Rowan
www.knitrowan.com
Fishnet Stockings, *Knitting the Perfect Pair*

Southwest Trading Company, Inc. (SWTC Inc.)
www.soysilk.com
Cabled Gloves, Fringed Scarf, Hat and Soul, *Freeform Style*

The Fibre Company
207.282.0734
www.thefibreco.com
Earflap Hat, *Closely Knit*

Knitting Glossary

beg	BEGINNING	inc	INCREASE	sc	SINGLE CROCHET
BO	BIND OFF	k	KNIT	SKP	SLIP, KNIT, PASS
C4F	CABLE 4 FRONT	kfb	KNIT 1 FRONT	sl	SLIP
C4B	CABLE 4 BACK		AND BACK	sm	SLIP MARKER
ch	CHAIN	k2tog	KNIT 2 TOGETHER	ssk	SLIP, SLIP, KNIT
cn	CABLE NEEDLE	m1	MAKE ONE	st(s)	STITCH(ES)
CO	CAST ON	p	PURL	St st	STOCKINETTE STITCH
dc	DOUBLE CROCHET	pm	PLACE MARKER	tog	TOGETHER
dec	DECREASE	psso	PASS SLIPPED	tbl	THROUGH BACK LOOP
DPN(s)	DOUBLE-POINTED		STITCH OVER	WS	WRONG SIDE
	NEEDLES	rem	REMAINING	w&t	WRAP AND TURN
est	ESTABLISHED	RS	RIGHT SIDE	wyib	WITH YARN IN BACK
foll	FOLLOWING	rnd	ROUND	wyif	WITH YARN IN FRONT
hdc	HALF DOUBLE CROCHET	rep	REPEAT	yo	YARN OVER

Index

Keep knitting!

Find more fabulous patterns in these great titles from F+W Media, Inc.

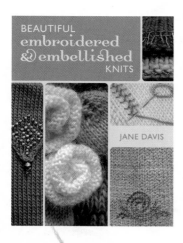

Beautiful Embroidered & Embellished Knits
by Jane Davis

Why settle for ordinary when you can create true originals? Learn how to make 31 fabulously detailed pieces—without the complex color sequences and tricky texture patterns that tend to take all the fun out of knitting. Simply knit the project in easy Stockinette stitch, then embellish with embroidery, beading, fringe and more. It's like icing on your knitted cake!

ISBN-10: 0-89689-809-1
ISBN-13: 978-0-89689-809-7
paperback, 128 pages, Z2916

Closely Knit
Handmade Gifts for the Ones You Love
by Hannah Fettig

Closely Knit is filled with thoughtful knitted gifts to fit all the people you love: special handknits for mothers, daughters, sisters, the men in your life, precious wee ones and treasured friends. Projects range from quick and simple to true labors of love, and each is rated with a handy time guide so you can choose what to knit based on how much time you have. Bonus quick-fix options will save the day when you need to whip up a meaningful gift in a jiffy.

ISBN-10: 1-60061-018-8
ISBN-13: 978-1-60061-018-9
paperback, 144 pages, Z1280

Felting The Complete Guide
by Jane Davis

Felting The Complete Guide is your definitive answer to felting, no matter what the question. With 35+ projects and a separate section devoted to a variety of felting techniques, this book is a felting resource that you will be able to turn to for years to come! Projects range in size and difficulty, from an easy ball to a knit vest, plus project variations show how basic felting techniques can be applied to other forms of art.

ISBN-10: 0-89689-590-4
ISBN-13: 978-0-89689-590-4
hardcover, 256 pages, Z1479

Freeform Style
Blend Knit & Crochet to Create Fiber Art Wearables
by Jonelle Raffino and Prudence Mapstone

Learn how to incorporate freeform knit and crochet into ten simple patterns, provided in three skill levels. Beginners will follow a written pattern and learn to incorporate one simple freeform element. Intermediate knitters will follow instructions for adding more elaborate freeform elements. The advanced fiber artist will learn to completely break away from the pattern to create an entirely freeform piece.

ISBN-10: 1-60061-138-9
ISBN-13: 978-1-60061-138-4
hardcover, 144 pages, Z2320